Huadong: The Story of a Chinese People's Commune

*Huadong: The Story of a Chinese
People's Commune*
Gordon Bennett

This topical and concise report on one commune in China's innovative commune system is designed to present key features of the system as a whole. The range of source materials—collected as a project of the Texas China Council and the University of Texas Center for Asian Studies— includes official Chinese documents, criticisms of a prominent regional leader published during the Cultural Revolution, official statements to foreign visitors at Huadong, observations about the commune by foreign visitors and journalists, and recollections by local emigrés. The author emphasizes the personal views of commune residents, and calls attention to important changes over the last few years. The sixty-five photographs included in the book give a vivid sense of everyday life at Huadong.

An introductory essay on the concept of the commune in Chinese Communist Party policy is followed by chapters covering Huadong's government and politics, economy, society, and culture. The conclusion points to likely developments in the future.

Gordon Bennett, associate professor of government at the University of Texas at Austin, is a specialist in Chinese politics. He has interviewed Chinese emigrés in Hong Kong during 1967-1969 and in 1975, and traveled in the People's Republic of China in 1976. Dr. Bennett is author of *Yundong: Mass Campaigns in Chinese Communist Leadership* (1976) and *China's Finance and Trade: A Policy Reader* (1978).

Huadong: The Story of a Chinese People's Commune

Gordon Bennett

with Ken Kieke and Ken Yoffy
Foreword by Sarah Weddington

Westview Press • Boulder, Colorado

Dawson • Folkestone, England

This volume is included in Westview's Special Studies on China and East Asia.

Copyright © 1978 by Westview Press

Published in 1978 in the United States of America by
    Westview Press, Inc.
    5500 Central Avenue
    Boulder, Colorado 80301
    Frederick A. Praeger, Publisher

Published in 1978 in Great Britain by
    Wm. Dawson and Sons, Ltd.
    Cannon House
    Folkestone
    Kent CT19 5EE England

Library of Congress Catalogue Card Number: 78-5025
ISBN (U.S.):0-89158-094-8 (hardcover)
ISBN (U.S.):0-89158-095-6 (paperback)
ISBN (U.K.):0-7129-8070-0 (hardcover)
ISBN (U.K.):0-7129-0882-X (paperback)

Printed and bound in the United States of America

To my airen, *Carol*

Contents

Tables, Figures, and Maps

Plates

Foreword

One of the most interesting and thought-provoking experiences during my service as a member of the Texas State Legislature was spending sixteen days in China in 1977 as part of a delegation sponsored by the National Committee on U.S.–China Relations. During the trip I had an opportunity to study the agricultural endeavors of the country, including a visit to a people's commune. What I saw there was much more than a large collective farm. It was an integrated community dedicated to two broad goals—first, to raising agricultural production, and second, as the Chinese say, to "serving the interests of the individual, the collective, and the state." In communes like the one I visited, most farming tasks are performed cooperatively by whole villages of people in commonly owned fields. But in addition, communes manufacture and repair farm machinery, construct water control and hydroelectric projects, sponsor agricultural experimentation, introduce new technology, and provide farm credit. Orderly marketing of each crop is ensured by a local "supply and marketing cooperative" whose prices are neither higher in lean years nor lower when the harvest is plentiful.

Noneconomic activities of communes are also remarkable. Child care facilities are widely available to preschool children. In education, six years of primary school is available to all children, and a few years more of middle school is open to many. Training in agricultural science and technology is offered to full-time students, as well as to older farmers in short courses. In health, there is an expanding system of rural hospitals, clinics, paramedics, and medical insurance plans, and Chinese traditional medicine is actively practiced. Prices for Western drugs are low. Most daily necessities can be bought by commune members at nearby cooperative stores. Shortages often occur, but market conditions are stable overall. Almost no luxury items are available. Other essential activities in the commune include fire fighting, police protection, sports events, cultural performances, festival celebrations, and, of course, politics. The commune is the deepest level of local government in China's countryside, and offices of several national agencies, such as the People's Bank and Ministry of Public Security, are found in commune towns.

All this adds up to a novel way of organizing rural society, and one that may have significant lessons for other developing countries where farms are still as small and labor-intensive as China's were a generation ago. Now that the improvement of food supplies to undernourished people in the world's poorer lands is gaining global recognition as one of the leading issues of our times, I think it is even more important to understand the distinctive strengths and weaknesses of China's commune approach. Moreover, China is achieving increasing importance as a world power, and the commune is part of the economic fabric of that power.

A good place to start toward developing an understanding of China and the commune system is this excellent case study of the Huadong People's Commune. Professor Bennett and his two student collaborators at the University of Texas at Austin have exhaustively pursued every accessible bit of information about Huadong. The result is a thorough examination, profusely illustrated, of all facets of life in a single Chinese commune. Specialists and nonspecialists alike will appreciate the authors' concise presentation of relevant detail. The report is well organized and written in an easy-to-read style.

The authors consistently cast critical eyes upon their subject. While their study indicates an attitude of great respect for Chinese rural achievements under Communist Party leadership, the work is no paean to peasant life since the revolution. Their evaluation of Chinese rural policies stems from a longstanding interest in the dramatic confrontation between age-old problems of poverty and exploitation in China on the one hand, and revolutionary solutions on the other.

In current Chinese thinking, collective farms are an intermediate stage of ownership in the historical transition to communism. Only some day in the distant future, when the country is much more advanced economically and politically, will it be possible for China to realize the goal of complete state ownership of farms. In the meantime, in China's view, people's communes are a necessary compromise between utopia and backwardness.

Sarah Weddington
General Counsel
U.S. Department of Agriculture
Washington, D.C.

Preface

This study is a joint project of the China Council of The Asia Society and the Texas China Council affiliated with the Center for Asian Studies at the University of Texas.* The China Council is a national program for adult public education on Chinese affairs, providing outreach through regional councils and collaborative projects, a variety of media-related activities, and a series of studies on modern Chinese history and China's role in the contemporary world. Major funding of the Council, and through it of the Texas China Council, is provided by The National Endowment for the Humanities with matching support from private foundations including The Rockefeller Foundation, The Henry Luce Foundation, and the Rockefeller Brothers Fund. The views expressed by the author are not necessarily those of The Asia Society, the China Council, the Texas China Council, or the members and sponsors of these programs.

The idea for the study originated with a suggestion by James Townsend in September 1976 that the China Council think about producing a set of materials for adult public education on the operation and importance of Chinese communes. Later that fall I proposed that the new Texas China

*The Asia Society, 133 East 58th Street, New York, New York 10022; the Texas China Council, 310 Student Services Building, Austin, Texas 78712.

Council take on this task as one of its opening projects. Charles Greer, my colleague in geography at Texas, who had visited Huadong Commune in 1974, suggested that a case study of Huadong Commune might serve as a vehicle for accomplishing the broader purpose. Initially, I employed one University of Texas student in oriental languages, Ken Kieke, as a research assistant on the project. Early in 1977 we were joined by a second student, Ken Yoffy, a volunteer from our course on Chinese politics. The two Kens proved indispensable at every stage. They collected and organized data, cross-indexed and tabulated facts and figures, selected photographs, undertook endless irregular tasks, drafted chapters, and spent hours consulting with me on the substance and design of our report. Ken Kieke drew all five maps. It is with the two of them in mind that I use the collective "we" below.

It is often asserted in modern Chinese studies that the method is the message. Analysts who read Chinese media for export tend to absorb the current official interpretations of all developments. Observers who visit China for a few weeks tend to accumulate favorable first impressions without ever having an opportunity to know anybody. Scholars who interview refugees in Hongkong tend to form a picture of China as a surprisingly diverse society about which few generalizations hold. Other sources produce other biases. We believe our study of Huadong is strengthened by the availability of several sources. Anna Louise Strong, an American journalist long resident in China, visited Huadong in 1962 and wrote about the commune in her book *The Rise of the Chinese People's Communes—and Six Years After* (Peking: Foreign Languages Press, 1964, pp. 175-181). Derek Davies, editor of the *Far East Economic Review*, visited Huadong in 1964 and published the results of his fact-finding in that journal on December 17, 1964 (pp. 564-567). During China's "Cultural Revolution" of 1966-1969, a Red Guard group investigated the transformation of Huadong into a model commune by a powerful regional official, Tao Zhu, and had its criticisms carried in a leading Guangzhou (Canton) newspaper, the *Nanfang ribao* (July 26, 1967; translated by the U.S. Consulate General at Hongkong in its *Survey of China Mainland Magazines,* No. 4011, pp. 14-23). Both Strong and Davies were at Huadong while Tao Zhu was still active in the commune's affairs.

Several years later, between 1971 and 1975, at least five delegations paid brief visits to Huadong, most of them for a day. About two hours in the morning would be taken up with welcoming speeches by host officials and an introduction to the work of the commune. The remainder of the day would be devoted to a guided tour of selected villages and enterprises. The opening statements would give information that the Chinese thought to be important, and sometimes would include a few more items that they thought might hold special interest for their guests. But since the area is close to Hongkong, from which most visitors entered China at the time, delegations typically found themselves at Huadong on their first or second day in China. This meant that the Chinese side had had little time to learn about their guests' special interests. It also meant that the visitors were less aggressive in their questioning, because they had yet to acquire a "feel" for China and for the etiquette of various social encounters. Despite these obstacles, some delegations managed to collect copious notes and photographs. Our procedure was first to accumulate the published reports of each delegation, then to solicit copies of original notes from individual delegation members, and finally to open correspondence with people who we thought might be able to make corrections or clarifications. Several persons very graciously supplied unpublished material or wrote us detailed letters, all of which raised our understanding far above the level possible from printed sources alone. Next we sent forty copies of our first draft manuscript to people who had visited Huadong, as well as to other scholars engaged in research on rural affairs in contemporary China. Most of them responded with valuable criticism and editorial suggestions, and in a few cases very detailed ones. We would be the first to agree that data based on a single visit of only a few hours is superficial. We hope that by carefully sifting and comparing the many reports from Huadong, and by subjecting our reconstruction to extensive review, we have been able to assemble a reasonably accurate account.

The first group to visit in the 1970s was a friendship delegation of the Committee of Concerned Asian Scholars. Its visit on July 24, 1971, occurred at the very beginning of the thaw in U.S.–Chinese relations. Their report appears as part of their collective book *China! Inside the People's Republic* (Bantam Books, 1972). They were followed by the New York State Educators' Study Group, which visited Huadong in July 1973 at the start of the anti-Confucius campaign, and one month before the Tenth Congress of the Chinese Communist Party (CCP). One member of that group, Ward Morehouse, contributed "Notes on Hua-tung Commune" to the *China Quarterly*, no. 67 (July-September 1976): 582-596. Three other members, L. Heidi Hursh, Robert Neiderberger, and Elaine Zanicchi, helped prepare an informative guide for ninth grade social studies, *Teaching about the People's Republic of China*, published in 1975 by the New York State Education Department. Two groups followed in 1974, one French and one American. M. Claude Aubert's group visited Huadong in March. His French article in *Espirit* (June 1974) appears in English translation in the *New Left Review*, no. 89 (January-February 1975): 86-96. The U.S. Water Resources Delegation went to Huadong on August 21, 1974. Their report, *Hydraulic Engineering and Water Resources in the People's Republic of China*, prepared by James E. Nickum, was published by the United States–China Relations Program at Stanford University. The latest visit to Huadong, at the time of this writing, has been an individual research trip by British sociologist Elisabeth J. Croll, who was able to conduct intensive interviews among families of Linong Brigade for several days in April 1977. The results appear in her article, "Chiang Village: A Household Survey," *China Quarterly,* no. 72 (December 1977):786-814.

It was possible to cross-check some of our data against the recollections of a Chinese student now living in the United States. He and his classmates had spent several months at Huadong. Another individual interviewed by John Burns had led a work team in 1964 to carry out the "Four Clean-ups" campaign at Huadong. Both interviews served to firm up some of our impressions.

Given the nature of this project, our debts to individuals are many. Andrew Nathan, who benefited from a three-day visit with the New York State Educators' Study Group, must be singled out, nevertheless. He often seemed to us two people, each with four hands. His notes came to eighteen single-spaced typewritten pages when transcribed, and scarcely a paragraph in our story is not informed by some detail or perspective captured by him. What is more, he managed to find time to shoot more than 100 excellent photographs, several of which are reproduced here. Claude Aubert has added an important dimension with his meticulous care for method and reliability. Not only does his article review important statistical assumptions, but he wrote us detailed letters delving further into these points. Bob Neiderberger kindly duplicated 253 of his slides of Huadong, including valuable maps, and gave us permission to reproduce a large number of his photographs. Ward Morehouse sent material that he had not included in his article. In correspondence with us, Kay Ann Johnson of the Committee of Concerned Asian Scholars friendship delegation offered many useful ideas about the role of women at Huadong. She also sent copies of original notes recorded by her, Paul Pickowicz, and Susan Shirk. James Nickum's observations led to important improvements in the economic sections of the manuscript. Leo Orleans sent material that led us to revise our population assumptions, reinforcing important criticisms communicated by Judith Banister. Paul Levine typed his handwritten notes for our convenience. William Parish,

Martin Whyte, Marc Blecher, Kim Woodard, Peggy Blumenthal, Robert Oxnam, Terry Lautz, Richard Bush, Joel Glassman, and Samuel Chu, all of whom read the draft manuscript and offered comprehensive suggestions, will easily recognize many passages that reflect their thoughtfulness. Richard Baum, Fred Crook, Joyce Kallgren, Diane Li, Helen Keller, Victor Li, John Burns, Raymond Ling, Yeung Sai Cheung, Yeung Sau Lun, Rhea Whitehead, Ray Whitehead, John McCoy, Pauline Ng, Carol Bennett, and others who offered valuable criticisms and suggestions on specific points merit our equal appreciation. Ying-kit Ng drew Figure 5.2. A great many fine editorial suggestions were given by Mervyn Adams Seldon, consulting editor for Westview Press and for Dawson Publishing in the United Kingdom, herself an able student of modern China. *Huadong* is their book too. We never could have done it alone. Responsibility for all inadequacies, however, is mine alone.

All current American dollar figures in the text are half of the reported Chinese yuan amounts, even though in reality the yuan/dollar exchange rate has fluctuated within a range slightly below a two-to-one ratio. Readers interested in knowing original rounded current yuan amounts need only multiply by two.

The name Huadong in standard Mandarin is pronounced differently than most English-speaking readers would guess. The *ua* in H*ua* rhymes with the *ua* in ig*ua*na. The *o* in d*o*ng rhymes with the *oo* in l*oo*k. Neither syllable is accented.

All Chinese names and terms are romanized with the "phonetic" (*pinyin*) system introduced by Chinese linguists in the 1950s. The new system has been slow to take hold in the West, because no major dictionary has employed it, because people antagonistic to the Communist government have not been willing to use it, and not least of all, because official Chinese publications themselves have used a mixture of three systems. The movement toward uniform adoption of *pinyin* is welcome, in our view, to reduce the confusion of multiple systems. Throughout the text we use *pinyin* consistently, even though many familiar names and places may look uneven though many familiar names and places may look unfamiliar with their new spellings. A few examples are listed on page xxxi. We made exceptions only for the word China (Zhongguo in *pinyin*), for names of places outside the People's Republic such as Hongkong (Xianggang), and for footnotes and bibliographic citations, where we have preserved original spellings for readers' convenience in reference.

Gordon Bennett
Austin, Texas

Pinyin Romanization of
Familiar Names

Pinyin	Familiar
Beijing *Bei* sounds like "*bay*"	Peking
cun	ts'un (village)
dazibao	ta-tzu-pao (big character poster)
Duan Wu Jie *Duan* like "*Juan*" *Wu* like "*wo*mb" *Jie* like "*jet*"	Tuan Wu Chieh (Dragon Boat Festival)
Guangdong *Gua*ng like "*Gua*m," d*ong* like "*Jung*"	Kwangtung
Guangzhou *zhou* like "*Joe*"	Canton
Hongqi H*ong* like "*Jung*" *qi* like "Apa*che*"	Hung-ch'i (*Red Flag*)

Huadong   Hua-tung
  H*ua* like "*Guam*"
  d*ong* like "J*ung*"

Jiang Qing   Chiang Ch'ing
  Jiang like "*John*"
  Qing like "*ching*-a-ling"

jin   chin (catty, 0.5 kilogram)

Jiuwantan   Chiu-wan-t'an
  Jiu like "*Joe*"
  wan like "*wan*d"
  tan like "*ton*sil"

Liuqi He   Liu-ch'i Ho
  Liu like "*Leo*"   (Liu-ch'i River)
  qi like "Apa*che*"
  he like "*h*ook"

Mao Zedong   Mao Tse-tung
  Mao like "*mou*nd"
  Ze like "bir*ds*"
  d*ong* like "J*ung*"

Qing Ming   Ch'ing Ming
  Qing like "*ching*-a-ling"

Tao Zhu   T'ao Chu
  Tao like "*tow*el"
  Zhu like "*Ju*dea"

xiang   hsiang
                                             (administrative village)

Xiangshanjiao   Hsiang-shan-chiao
   Xi like *"see"*
   Xiang like "beyond"
   shan like "chanteuse"
   jiao like "jowel"

Zhou Enlai   Chou En-lai
   Zhou like "*Joe*"
   En like "undo"
   lai like "lye"

Huadong: The Story of a Chinese People's Commune

1
The Importance of Communes
in Contemporary China

The study of a country's economic and political systems is all too often the study of institutions—banks, industries, political parties, congresses, and committees—or of presidents, prime ministers, and chairmen. It is sometimes hard to see how these institutions or top leaders relate to the day-to-day affairs of individuals' lives and the real world in which they live. One solution to the problem is to study how a community or an institution works for its members, and how it interacts with other government levels. In China, the commune, an agricultural collective, is a particularly appropriate choice for this kind of study, for it is the administrative level at which the government speaks loudest to China's farm families, and also the level at which China's farmers speak loudest to higher authorities. Since the rural population living on communes is about 75 to 80 percent of China's total population, the commune is a very important institution indeed. This book focuses on Huadong Commune in Guangdong Province on China's southern coast, both because Huadong resembles other Chinese communes in important ways, and because it has been possible to collect a good deal of information about it from visitors, former residents, and documentary sources. Like China's other communes, it was established in 1958 and has changed greatly in the intervening years. Before examining its history and studying the

PLATE 1. Power lines pass small village on Liuqi River near Huadong Commune. (Charles Greer)

many facets of commune life, a few words are in order about the role of the communes in China's development strategy.

China's Development Strategy and the Communes

China's economic achievements under communist rule have been impressive, in all likelihood surpassing what the country could have achieved under a less disciplined regime in peacetime. The government has attained a very high investment rate, leading to an overall growth rate that has averaged about 6 percent per year since 1949. Such growth has been heavily dependent on food and other agricultural products. In food production alone, the annual growth rate of about 2 percent since 1949 has slightly exceeded population growth, which most authoritative observers estimate at something less than 2 percent per year. This slow but sure rise in per capita food production represents important progress over the prewar period, for little real growth in per capita food supply seems to have occurred in the decades before the communist regime took power.

China's most important rural achievements, though, lie

behind these statistics. The Chinese development strategy includes the countryside as well as the city, in hopes of overcoming the rural-urban disparities in growth and living conditions that typically plague industrializing countries early on. Many Chinese policies have been designed to advance the rural economy and to improve the standard of living in small towns and villages. Population growth has been contained. Everyone who wants to work can find some type of job. Taxes are low and administered fairly. Prices are stable, and rationing of items in short supply attempts to control hoarding and speculation. Most farm children finish primary school —a rarity in the prewar period. Rural people have access to hospitals and cooperative health insurance plans. Cultural life in the countryside is expanding. Life in China's villages today is certainly not easy, for agricultural labor is still very hard work and amenities are relatively few. What is important is the improvement over earlier times.

This transformation of Chinese agriculture and rural life has attracted much attention in other countries. The great majority of people in Third World countries live in rural settings not unlike China's villages. People there are seriously examining the "Chinese model" of development in search of better solutions for their own problems of poverty. The so-called Chinese model is not a single set of consistent prescriptions. It began in the 1950s with China's imitations of Soviet economic strategies: (1) nationalization of the means of production in industry; (2) the collectivization of agriculture; (3) the mobilization of the state and population by means of a Leninist party; and (4) a "big push" industrialization effort as a central economic policy objective.[1] But as Chinese and Soviet paths diverged toward the end of the decade, distinctively Maoist approaches also began to appear: (5) a greater emphasis on the economic development of rural areas, in which communes, small industries, and a high priority for agriculture figure prominently; (6) more encouragement for decentralized development and planning carried out within a context of local self-reliance; (7) a more egalitarian outlook that seeks to reduce economic and social differentials throughout the society; (8) a greater emphasis on nonmaterial and collective work incentives; (9) a greater effort to mobilize the masses behind political themes; and (10) a strategy of economic development through radical experimentation, struggle, and leaps, rather than through gradual, orderly, and familiar methods.[2] After Chairman Mao's death in September 1976, and especially after the arrest a few weeks later of the "gang of four" leaders who had been closely associated with the Chairman, previous policies came under review once again. The late 1970s saw a return to many of the Chinese strategies of the 1950s, with the Maoist modifications of the intervening years under active reconsideration.

Chinese communes have reflected these changes in development strategy. Initially a wholly novel experiment involving a utopian level of communal living and production, they now practice the art of the possible. The big and centralized institutions of the late 1950s have become smaller and decentralized. Early impulses to "leap forward" into communism have given way to a healthy respect for a limited amount of private property during a long period of gradual transition to communism.

Are the communes an essential element of the "Chinese model" of development? Is the institution exportable alone, or only as part of a total development strategy? Unfortunately, we can only speculate whether China's successful development strategy is divisible and transferable elsewhere part by part. Some scholars analyze China's success as a combination of factors—intensive revolution, tight one-party rule, ideological unity, mass campaign style of leadership, and egalitarian ideals under socialism—which are effective only together, not separately. Other scholars are willing to entertain the possibility that the Chinese form of some institutions, such as communes, might take root in other developing countries independently of other aspects of Beijing's development strategy. Only time will tell. At the very least, the Chinese experience shows the world what poor rural communities can accomplish in the late twentieth century, even though we do not yet understand the means required.

Antecedents of the Chinese Commune

The Chinese commune, for all of its novel features, has historical roots. Western history, for example, records many forms of collective institutions dating back to the fall of the Roman Empire. Rome itself, Flanders, Avignon, and Barcelona are four examples. Since the eighteenth century, the term commune has often had revolutionary, utopian, or religious connotations. A prime example was the Paris Commune formed by urban workers and small tradesmen during the French Revolution. In 1871, a new Paris Commune was organized by Marxists and followers of several French socialists in order to oppose a humiliating peace with Prussia after the Franco-Prussian War. In the United States, followers of Charles Fourier established experimental utopian communes at West Roxbury, Massachusetts (Brook Farm), and Red Bank, New Jersey (the North American Phalanx), among other places. A number of religious groups did the same, generally with more success. All these early creations, however, were alien presences in their social surroundings, because their principles diverged sharply from those of their feudal or capitalist hosts. Until the twentieth century, they were little more than sideshows.

A new and more serious stage emerged when governments began to sponsor communes instead of ridiculing them. The first to do so was the Soviet Union, when it established the *kolkhoz* (collective farm) in 1929. By 1972, there were 32,300 *kolkhozy*, each one having an average of 7,500 acres under cultivation. These tend to be larger in area, if smaller in population, than the average Chinese commune. Other prominent experience comes from Israel, in the form of the *moshav ovdim* (workers' settlement), the *moshav shitufi* (a modified collective), and the more famous *kibbutz* (commune). About 5 percent of Israel's population hold membership in 300-odd *kibbutzim,* leasing land owned by the Jewish National Fund in the name of the Jewish people.

The Chinese *renmin gongshe* (people's commune) does not look much like earlier experiments abroad, for it evolved out of Chinese conditions as well as Marxist ideals. Before collective organizations could be formed in the countryside, the Chinese communists first had to break the hold of the landowning classes. Early experiments in land reform were carried out in communist base areas from the late 1920s through the war with Japan (1937-1945) and the Civil War (1946-1949), and then throughout the country after Liberation in 1949. The next step, taken in the mid-1950s, was to encourage the peasants to work together to increase production through the formation, first, of "mutual aid teams" and, later, of small "agricultural producers' cooperatives" (APCs). Elementary APCs were followed by larger and more advanced ones, but even advanced ones experienced severe problems stemming from differences in members' wealth and in their attitudes toward work. It was time for new initiatives.

Emergence of the Chinese Communes

By 1957, China had recovered from the ravages of the Sino-Japanese War and the Civil War. The Chinese Communist Party had consolidated its power, and the country had made important economic advances during the course of its first five-year plan (1953-1957). After eight years of communist rule, China's rural people were aware of many changes in their lives. China better controlled its destiny in world affairs. Coastal cities no longer needed to tolerate the offensive presence of privileged Westerners and Japanese. Life security was greater: most people enjoyed steady work, regular food supply, stable prices, and protection against natural disasters, even if newspaper descriptions of current prosperity then seemed unduly rosy. For most Chinese, political authority was more visible, even though at times actions of local leaders were still impossible to understand. Waves of mass campaigns had mobilized millions of people to accomplish great feats of public improvement and construction, but these same campaigns often consisted of tiresome "mass line" rituals publicly denouncing "rightism," "localism," or other deviant tendencies. One inner voice told people to be active in politics because many Communist Party programs worked to their benefit. Another inner voice, however, counseled passivity, because a change in line might leave activists on the wrong side of an issue where they would be vulnerable to criticism. Collective agriculture still struck many as an experiment; the two-year-old advanced APCs had internal conflicts and problems. Yet no one's experiences proved to be adequate preparation for the grand restructuring of rural life about to descend upon China's villages—the change to people's communes.

Beginning in at least 1956 with the debate over a draft "1956-1967 National Program for Agricultural Development," various proposals were put forward to turn the advanced coops into more integrated rural communities, instead of purely economic units. But China's leaders were not agreed on a solution to the crisis of the advanced APCs. Some believed that the advanced coops of about 200 families each were too large and favored returning to the earlier size based on natural villages (*cun*) of just twenty to thirty families. Other Party members, following the lead of Chairman Mao Zedong, believed that the key to modernizing the countryside lay in mechanized farming and in the construction of larger waterworks. To achieve this, they favored experimenting with even larger collective units.

Chairman Mao's side had the edge. The political atmosphere was "leftist." During the summer of 1957, a rural "socialist education campaign" had criticized local officials and others in positions of responsibility ("cadres" in Chinese parlance) for failing to appreciate the value of advanced socialist institutions and policies. At the same time, in a "transfer downward" campaign, hundreds of thousands of state cadres in urban posts were sent to new assignments in rural towns and cooperatives. The intent of this campaign apparently was threefold: to remove "right"-leaning cadres from higher levels of state organization, to raise the quality of administrative personnel at the lowest levels, and, by bringing in outsiders, to overcome the tendency of local cadres to identify too strongly with local interests. At the conclusion of this antirightist campaign late in 1957, Chairman Mao traveled to several provinces to supervise the purges of provincial leaders whose conservative ideas he had opposed. Other campaigns added to the momentum. Beginning in late 1957, huge corvées were mobilized to build important flood control and other waterworks (many projects being much too big for advanced coops to undertake.) A "two oppositions" campaign early in 1958 equated opposition to waste with opposition to conservatism. Other campaigns pressed for great leaps in agricultural production and in the creation of small industries. A key characteristic of the "Great Leap Forward" of 1958, formally launched in May, was ever-escalating aims in every field of endeavor—economic, cultural, military, and others. Left and right deviations from the Party line were equally wrong, but by the summer of 1958 people had little difficulty agreeing that "erring to the left is better than erring to the right" (*ning zuo wu you*), and the pace of change accelerated. During the spring, a few localities had reported successful mergers of APCs. The enlarged Weixing (Sputnik) APC of Suiping County, Henan Province, for example, incorporated twenty small APCs on April 20, 1958. After adding seven more APCs in late June, Weixing had 9,369 member households. In July, it was acclaimed as China's first "commune"—the first use of the expression. Chinese leaders had apparently taken the term from the Paris

Commune of 1871, a symbolic event in world Marxism.[3]

This development suited Chairman Mao's purposes well. He had become intrigued with several experiments conducted with larger agricultural units, especially ones including plans for local industrial development and militia organization. He had visited and commented upon several of these trial units and was impressed in particular with Qiliying Commune in Henan Province, the site of his widely publicized visit on August 6, 1958.[4] Shortly thereafter, Mao's almost casual remark—"It is better to set up people's communes: they have the advantage of integrating agriculture, industry, trade, education, and militia and are easier to lead"—was headlined in *People's Daily,* the official newspaper of the CCP Central Committee. Some localities, responding immediately to the Chairman's published remark, prepared to shift to the commune form of organization. Other localities waited for the Party's formal "Resolution on the Establishment of People's Communes in Rural Areas," which was passed on August 29. In either case, provincial and local cadres, picking up the cue to lean to the "left," gave extreme interpretations to every informal or formal signal. The following passage in the resolution, and others like it, encouraged such "left" behavior by suggesting that China would be first in the world to arrive at full communism (ownership of the means of production by the people as a whole).

> Collective ownership in people's communes already contains some elements of ownership by the people as a whole. These elements will grow constantly in the course of the continuous development of people's communes and will gradually replace collective ownership. The transition from collective ownership to ownership by the people as a whole is a process, the completion of which may take less time—three or four years—in some places, and longer—five or six years or even longer—elsewhere. Even with the completion of this transition, people's communes, like state-owned industry, are still socialist in character, where the principle of "from each according to

ability and to each according to labor" prevails. After a
number of years, as the social product increases greatly, the
Communist consciousness and morality of the entire people
are raised to a much higher degree, and universal education is
instituted and developed, the differences between workers and
peasants, town and country, and mental and manual labor—
legacies of the old society that have inevitably been carried
over into the socialist period—and the remnants of unequal
bourgeois rights which are the reflection of these differences—
will gradually vanish. Then the function of the state will be
limited to protecting the country from external aggression but
it will play no role internally. At that time Chinese society will
enter the era of Communism, when the principle of "from
each according to ability and to each according to need" will
be practiced.[5]

By the end of 1958, more than 26,000 communes incorporated nearly all of China's rural population. Many of these
had been put together so quickly that they were little more
than skeleton organizations.

The popular response to the transition to people's communes was marked by caution and skepticism. Those in
charge of village meetings to discuss the commune idea were
easily recognized as the "five big cadres" of the administrative village, or *xiang*—the Party branch secretary, the village
chief, the local public security officer, the militia chief, and
the Women's Association chairperson. To many, the economic benefits that these leaders promised sounded more distant
than immediate. The public debate over communes often was
not a real debate at all but a prepared script of contrasts
between the bright promises of moving forward to communal
life and the dark uncertainties of retreating to smaller
coops. People remained unconvinced by visionary talk. The
plan envisaged each commune as a huge unit composed of
many advanced coops. The commune was to be responsible
for industry, agriculture, finance, banking, retailing, education, and military affairs, as well as for all traditional functions of local government. It was unclear just what benefits

this "big and comprehensive" unit would bring. People from relatively well organized and prosperous advanced coops were upset at having to merge with other less successful communities.

After September, many people's worst fears were realized. The "five big cadres" and others eager to demonstrate their solidly "left" orientation followed the most extreme possible interpretation of every decision handed down. According to the Party Central Committee's August 29 resolution, coops were to merge into communes through a process of "ideological emancipation on a voluntary basis, without any compulsion." In fact, most people felt that they had little choice in the matter. The resolution said that mergers should occur gradually ("before or after autumn, in the coming winter or next spring") with care taken to adjust problems along the way. In fact, the organization of most communes was rushed through immediately. The resolution allowed flexibility in the handling of people's private property; it stated that a private household's garden plot "may be" turned over to collective management, that scattered fruit trees "for the time being may remain privately owned," and that the problem of each individual's contribution of funds to the coop "can be handled after a year or two." Other private property was not mentioned. In fact, cadres demanded not only that private plots and orchards be turned over to collective management immediately, but also that collectivization include individual houses, small tools, and even cooking utensils. One common regulation specified that existing substandard houses should be dismantled as soon as possible, the bricks, tiles, and lumber to be used to build new houses for which residents would pay rent to the commune. According to the resolution, "where conditions permit" the coop system of paying members according to days of work contributed "may be shifted" to a factory-type wage system. In fact, cadres were impatient to pay peasants as if they were industrial workers and were eager to begin implementing the communist principles "to each according to need." They wanted the income of each commune member to consist of only about 40 percent in wages and as much as 60 percent in free food and other necessities. They were proud to tell visitors that at their commune "one can eat without paying" (*chi fan buyao qian*).

More striking changes came at a dizzying pace. In some places individuals' bank deposits were confiscated to augment the commune's investment fund: after all, went the argument, with necessities freely supplied and rural markets closed, individuals should have little need for money. Extremely high construction and production targets were announced in the shrill language of battle: "armies" of workers would "fight" day and night to "win new victories" for the general line of building socialism. Lights were strung up with poles in the fields to enable "shock forces" to continue working after dark. At one point a call was issued to "fight round the clock, eating and sleeping beside the fields." Household chores were collectivized to free women for labor in the fields or in new commune industries. Nurseries cared for children, sewing teams mended clothes, and communal mess halls prepared meals for all. Some zealous cadres even collected household cooking pots and melted them down to help enforce required mess hall dining. Statements critical of the family unit were heard from persons in authority, and women were mobilized into the labor force. Ironically, all talk of overpopulation and birth control ceased, and "unemployment" became an unmentionable concept. Workers were recruited to man small commune factories for making tools and construction materials. Even crude grades of steel were produced in backyard furnaces. This frenzy of activity proved enormously fatiguing, and stories began to circulate of peasants who refused to work, slaughtered livestock rather than give it to the commune, or physically attacked cadres.

These early months of China's communes were even stranger than some of the fictions amazed outsiders wrote about them. From the perspective of two decades, however, it is intriguing to wonder if so massive a program could ever have been launched without political turbulence. Perhaps no one could have designed communes calmly, as an architect designs a building. Perhaps they could only have emerged out of a unique combination of circumstances—exaggerated optimism about the 1958 harvest, political uncertainty under Mao Zedong's aggressive leadership, rivalry with the Soviet Union about the correct road to communism and other issues, and the Party's historical experience with mass mobilization. Perhaps the best analogy for their emergence would be a new and modern city rising out of the ashes of war or the destruction of an earthquake. No one would argue that bombs or earthquakes are reasonable instruments of urban planning. Yet they may serve as the occasion for advances that would not otherwise have been possible.

Changes in Commune Structure, 1959-1962, and Today's Communes

The new Chinese communes of 1958 were experiments; initial setbacks in their operation engendered a sharp debate at top Party levels and led to extensive readjustment. By 1962, the communes had assumed a fairly stable form, the major elements of which persist today. First, they are rural. Urban communes were tried for a while but were abandoned. Second, they are organizational vehicles for strengthening and modernizing the collective rural economy. Not only do they support agriculture directly by acquiring and maintaining tractors, constructing water control systems, carrying out agricultural experiments, and providing a multitude of other services, but they also promote rural development through investing in the "five small industries" (cement, electric power, farm machinery, fertilizers, and iron and steel) as well as in other small-scale nonagricultural enterprises. Third, they are the lowest level of local government in the countryside. In addition to their economic functions, communes administer for their members schools, hospitals, banks, shops, police and fire protection, telephone exchanges, post offices, cultural and sports activities, radio and television rebroadcasting, and more.

Much popular literature on Chinese communes gives undue attention to their radical, experimental features during the Great Leap Forward in 1958. Critics are especially prone to overlook later adjustments (which, if they are mentioned at all, are usually described as "retreats" from "utopianism"). Yet these modifications of 1959-1961 are an essential part of the story, for they resulted in the sharp contrasts between the first communes and those of today.

Much of the 1959-1961 debate over the need for changes in commune structure was phrased in ideological terms. In 1958, the leadership had sought to reach communism by a Great Leap Forward. Since 1962, they have spoken of the present stage of history as one of transition from socialism (collective ownership of the means of production) to communism (state ownership, or ownership by the "whole people"). And they discuss the transition in far more cautious language than they did in 1958. As phrased in the General Program section of the new (1977) Communist Party Constitution: "Socialist society covers a historical period of considerable length. In this period classes, class contradictions and class struggle between the socialist road and the capitalist road and the danger of capitalist restoration invariably continue to exist."[6] Thus, once again, the stage of pure communism is seen as a long way off. In the interim, public policy is supposed to promote the interests of "the state, the collective, and the individual," not the state alone.

These ideological revisions have been reflected in commune life. Rural markets have revived. The family is honored once again as a desirable social institution. In today's communes, mess halls and most "free supply" items have disappeared. There are no more attempts to transform peasants immediately into wage-earning proletarians. Less is seen of "shock troop" approaches to rural labor organization, or of instantaneous solutions (such as irrational close planting) to the problem of slow growth in agricultural production. Gone also are backyard steel making, the reporting of inflated statistics, and the call "every man a soldier." Most noticeable of all, however, is the decentralization of administration and production below the commune level. Significant activities now are managed by smaller collective subunits, whose members have greater control over their work than in 1958.

After much adjustment and experimentation in the years following the Great Leap Forward, commune organization has shaken down to a "three-level system of ownership," under which specified decisions and functions are reserved to the two lower levels—production brigades and production teams. Not only are today's communes smaller by half than the early ones (more than 50,000 today have replaced the 26,000 of 1958), but the subordinate brigades and teams have become more significant. Today's communes are the lowest level of government administration. In that capacity, commune centers, usually in large market towns, have state personnel carrying out duties in banking, commerce, procurement of agricultural products, tax collections, and public security. At the same time, today's communes are the highest level of rural collective. Commune-run enterprises earn as much as one-third of all rural income. Communes take advantage of their large size to build irrigation canals, drainage ditches, hydroelectric power stations, hospitals, small industries, schools, and other facilities for their membership. They also promote modern farming techniques, the use of chemical fertilizer, electrification, and mechanization among teams in villages where modern methods are still strange and objects of suspicion. Commune managers generally are very competent individuals and usually have had some managerial training. Most communes have from 500 to 1,000 Communist Party members.

a

c

PLATE 2. *a*, *b*, and *c*: People and goods entering the commune town, Tuiguang, by foot, bicycle, cart, tractor, truck, and bus. (Robert

b

d

Neiderberger) *d*: Families market produce from their private plots in
the commune town. (Andrew Nathan)

Below the commune level are an average of fifteen "production brigades" (*shengchan da dui*), each with an average of 200 households or more, or about 1,000 people. In size, production brigades often closely resemble the old advanced APCs. Brigade leaders spend half their time performing administrative duties and half their time laboring in the fields. In the 1970s, brigades have been growing in importance, and more and more of them have been acquiring headquarters buildings. According to the leader of Huadong Commune's Linong Brigade, Jiang Lihe, brigade functions include: (1) helping teams make production plans and coordinating team production with the state economic plan, (2) supervising teams to insure fulfillment of plan targets, (3) guiding teams on the proper division of income between distribution to members and saving to develop production, (4) managing brigade water conservancy projects, and (5) providing services beyond the capacity of teams in such areas as militia, education, public health, and medium-sized agricultural machinery.

While today's production brigades give strong political leadership and support to their teams, they are not yet so autonomous in economic affairs. Few brigade-level enterprises earn very large profits; their role seems rather to be direct support of the teams. Common functions are tractor servicing, farm machine repair, electric power supply, animal husbandry, brick and tile making, and fish breeding. Ordinarily brigade enterprises earn less than one-sixth of all rural income. In large communes like Huadong, relatively few brigades seem to correspond to traditional village or marketing communities. As a result, there have only been cautious and scattered efforts to raise the "basic accounting unit" and the "basic ownership level" up to the brigade level. Recruiting competent brigade leadership is a problem in some places, and often brigade leaders seem to feel closer to their membership than they do to the commune leadership. Brigade leaders help resolve conflicts among member teams or villages. Most brigades have twenty-five or more Communist

Party members.

Brigades average seven production teams (*shengchan dui*) each, and each team generally has about thirty households, or roughly 150 people. Most production teams bring together the residents of one small village, the age-old, basic-level community of rural China. Some are single surname villages, or lineages, where village ties may be reinforced by kinship bonds. Team leadership is not even a half-time responsibility, and team "headquarters" may be no more than the team leader's home. Teams are the basic level in the "three-level system of ownership." Each team owns the land, forest, and water resources within its area (other than those managed by the state), as well as its draft animals, small farm machinery, and farm implements.[7] Teams are also the so-called basic accounting unit in rural China. This means that they organize their own production and distribution of income, handle their accounting, and are responsible for their own profits or losses. In other words, members of a team rise or fall together. No one family can prosper while other families in the same team with the same labor power do not. Thus, members of a team have a strong incentive to cooperate with each other to maximize their collective welfare, but a well-run team need not be overly concerned about a conflict-ridden team in the same brigade. Although production teams have an important degree of autonomy, they do receive political leadership and economic assistance from their brigade. Formally speaking, no one can make them plant cotton instead of grain if they absolutely refuse to do so, but realistically, teams do not exist in a political void. They can be their own masters only if they stubbornly insist on exercising their rights.

Today's production teams are the smallest and most tightly knit of China's collective organizations. Team members are often related or are at least friends or neighbors from the same village. Brigade members from different villages may remain strangers. Team members must decide collectively how many work points per day the labor of each individual is worth. They must assign collective tasks to each other. They must decide collectively how to respond to requests from the brigade and the commune. For example, the commune might want all teams to plant 10 percent more acres of winter wheat one year to build up the collective grain reserve, but team members may not comply if they believe that they will earn less cash income from winter wheat than they would if they continued to use those acres for vegetables. Or the commune might urge teams to apply more chemical fertilizer instead of simple manure, but team members may have to be convinced of the potential benefits —especially if they have not had to pay for fertilizer before. They have to maintain on-field waterworks, a granary, draft animals, and a few farm machines. Recruiting competent team leadership is a big problem everywhere, and teams that have a capable person or two who can manage all facets of team life consider themselves fortunate. Some teams have a few Party members, but many have none. Production teams are basic, but they cannot operate without assistance.

To carry out their tasks, teams subdivide into "work groups" (*zu*). Some are permanent (pig raising), and some are temporary (rice harvesting). The temporary groups rotate seasonal tasks (twenty days of transplanting followed by weeding, hoeing, insect killing, and other jobs). Ordinarily people choose their own work group, so these tend to be compatible groups of friends and relatives. How do individual households fare under this arrangement? China's 150 million rural families average about five members each. Ordinarily two or three of them would be rated as "full labor power" and be capable of earning a full share of the team's collective income. Families can supplement their collective share by selling produce from their own private plot or by selling home manufactures. Private economic activity might include raising pigs or chickens, growing vegetables, gathering medicinal herbs from a nearby forest, or making straw

a

b

PLATE 3. *a* and *b*: Production team members transplant rice seedlings in late July. (Robert Neiderberger)

sandals. Home-grown or homemade products are permitted on local markets only if a family member, not a middleman, does the selling. Prices on those markets are subject to some negotiation between seller and buyer but may never exceed boundaries set by the state and enforced by local "market control committees." About 20 percent of most rural families' income originates in this semiprivate sector. Probably more significant are the many welfare benefits individuals receive. These collective benefits include low-cost medical care, a cooperative medical insurance plan, almost free education for children through middle school, and distribution of food and other necessities, even during times of short supply, at low and stable prices. Moreover, numerous items are protected now as families' legitimate private property—most houses, all bank savings (either from earned income or from inheritance), everyday household goods, sewing machines, bicycles, items received from relatives overseas, and consumer goods such as cameras, radios, and wristwatches. Commune members would like to be more affluent and be able to consume more, but probably very few of them, if given the choice, would opt for a return to the prerevolutionary system of striking inequality.

Huadong People's Commune: How Typical Is It?

China is a country of extreme regional diversity. As a result, the original commune idea has taken many different local forms, and no commune anywhere is typical of all the others. Nevertheless, certain key features of commune life are fairly standard everywhere in China. Thus, a knowledge of the details of daily life in Huadong Commune can provide important insights into the operation of this crucial institution throughout the country.

Huadong People's Commune lies thirty miles north of Guangzhou, a major Chinese city (population almost 3 million) and the capital of Guangdong Province on China's southern coast. The Nanling Mountains, an east-west chain, separate the province from the rest of China. The area is a densely populated river plain, whereas many communes are found in more isolated or mountainous places. The province, which is approximately the size of Minnesota or West Germany, had a population of close to 43 million in the mid-1970s—twice that of California and nearly equal to that of England. Administratively, Huadong is a part of Hua County, which is considered part of greater Guangzhou Municipality. Nevertheless, county residents are treated differently in some respects than people living in counties closer to the city. Most importantly, perhaps, Hua County residents may not legally take jobs in Guangzhou City proper. Commune residents frequently bicycle into Guangzhou for shopping or recreation, however. They may also take the regularly scheduled bus, a trip of about an hour and a half. All but the last stretch is along paved roadway. The buses stop at the commune center, or headquarters, which is labeled on maps as Tuiguang, although local people still use an old name, Xiangshanjiao. Regular bus service also connects the commune with the county seat at Huaxian (old name Xinhua). The name Huadong, or "Hua East," refers to the commune's location at the eastern end of Hua County.

The region is one of abundant water. Three large rivers—the West, the North, and the East—drain the basin defined by the Nanling range. The broad alluvial plain formed at their confluence, known as the Pearl River Delta, consists of large areas of reclaimed farmland amid a 1,500-mile-long maze of shifting channels and canals. The commune lies on the north side of the Liuqi River on the edge of the delta. Its region is interlaced with waterways that allow ready irrigation, hydroelectric power, and convenient transportation by boat, in contrast to communes located on drier plains or steppes or in hilly regions without some of Huadong's geographic advantages. These silting waterways have been worked on continuously throughout the settled history of the region; it is

24

MAP I.I
PEARL RIVER DELTA

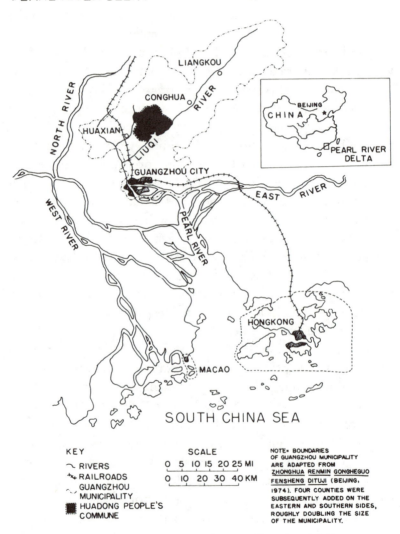

LIANGKOU

NORTH RIVER

CONGHUA

HUAXIAN

LIUQI RIVER

GUANGZHOU CITY

WEST RIVER

PEARL RIVER

EAST RIVER

CHINA
BEIJING
PEARL RIVER
DELTA

HONGKONG

MACAO

SOUTH CHINA SEA

KEY

∼ RIVERS
⊁ RAILROADS
GUANGZHOU
MUNICIPALITY
HUADONG PEOPLE'S
COMMUNE

SCALE

0 5 10 15 20 25 MI

0 10 20 30 40 KM

NOTE: BOUNDARIES
OF GUANGZHOU MUNICIPALITY
ARE ADAPTED FROM
ZHONGHUA RENMIN GONGHEGUO
FENSHENG DITUJI (BEIJING,
1974). FOUR COUNTIES WERE
SUBSEQUENTLY ADDED ON THE
EASTERN AND SOUTHERN SIDES,
ROUGHLY DOUBLING THE SIZE
OF THE MUNICIPALITY.

estimated today that man-made canals outnumber natural streams by two or three to one. Tree-lined dikes protect reclaimed areas from floodwaters.

Huadong's area is now 150 square kilometers (58 square miles)—a little larger than the city of San Francisco. The half of the land closest to the Liuqi River is low-lying plain with plenty of water. It is farmed by ethnic Chinese. The northern half is very hilly and is inhabited mostly by a much smaller number of people belonging to the Hakka minority (migrants from North China in an earlier historical period). Over the centuries, many local people have migrated overseas. Roughly one-fifth of the population of Guangdong Province is classified as "overseas Chinese," referring to people who have relatives among the 15 million or more Chinese living outside China in Southeast Asia (excluding Hongkong and Macao), Canada, the United States, or Europe. In Hua County, the proportion is slightly higher; a county official told one visitor to Huadong in 1962 that 65,000 (24 percent) of Hua County's currently registered population of 277,000 were "overseas Chinese." There are also some other facilities for these people. The nearby Huaqiao State Farm is tilled by 1,500 "overseas Chinese," most of whom returned home from Indonesia after the coup against Sukarno in 1965.

People in Huadong's region have had fairly intense contact with foreigners, including Western missionaries and traders in the nineteenth and twentieth centuries and Japanese soldiers during World War II. They receive news, money, and consumer goods from family members abroad. They enjoy visits, most commonly during the Qing Ming Festival, with relatives from Hongkong and Macao. They can pick up Hongkong radio stations, and the reception of Voice of America broadcasts is also clear. Thus, people in Huadong Commune, more than people from most villages elsewhere in China, are aware of facts and ideas from abroad. Perhaps not all foreign statements enjoy wide credibility. An example might be the Voice of America's Cold War–like contention in

TABLE 1.1

How Huadong People's Commune Compares with the National Average, 1973

Demographic Feature	Huadong (A)	National average (B)	Ratio A/B
Population	61,000	15,000	4.1
Cultivated acres	12,000	5,000	2.4
Number of brigades	20	15	1.3
Average persons per brigade	3,050	1,000	3.1
Number of teams	320	100	3.2
Average teams per brigade	15	7	2.1
Average people per team	191	150	1.3

1962 that American aid to India promotes "self-help" among peasants, resulting in the preservation of their "human dignity and freedom," a necessity that "those Red Chinese communes destroy."[8]

The Huadong standard of living is slightly above China's rural average, even though commune leaders modestly tell visitors, "We're still behind advanced communes." In the mid-1970s, 35 percent of its teams were rated as "advanced," 50 percent were "average," and 15 percent were "comparatively backward." Undoubtedly Huadong's most impressive achievement is its waterworks construction. In the old days, 80 percent of the hilly lands in the north were subject to drought, and 20 percent of lowlands in the south were vulnerable to flooding. According to one local saying, "Three days of sun start the water wheels turning; one day of rain brings flood." Thousands of peasants living in the lowlands had to labor at the backbreaking task of raising Liuqi River water up to the level of the fields. The "New Liuqi" Canal completed in 1959 (locally dubbed the *sheng-ming he* or "river of life") and the Liqi Dam completed in 1970 have brought 96 percent of the commune's cultivated

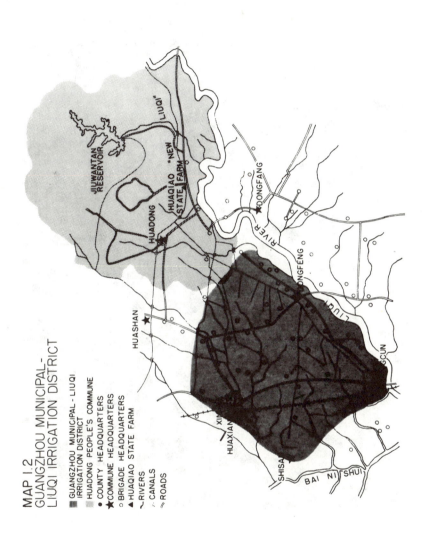

27

MAP I.2
GUANGZHOU MUNICIPAL-
LIUQI IRRIGATION DISTRICT

▓▓ GUANGZHOU MUNICIPAL - LIUQI
▒▒ IRRIGATION DISTRICT
▒▒ HUADONG PEOPLE'S COMMUNE
● COUNTY HEADQUARTERS
★ COMMUNE HEADQUARTERS
○ BRIGADE HEADQUARTERS
▲ HUAQIAO STATE FARM
⌇ RIVERS
⌐ CANALS
═ ROADS

a

PLATE 4. *a*: Jiuwantan reservoir pumphouse. (Charles Greer) *b*: Five Finger Mountain hydroelectric plant at Liangkou Commune near Huadong. (Charles Greer) *c*: Raised aqueduct at Huadong. (Charles Greer)

b

c

land under gravity-feed irrigation (no pumps required). Triple cropping (three harvests per year) is practiced. Of the acreage normally sown to grain, Huadong farmers plant early rice on nearly 80 percent, late rice on nearly 90 percent, and barley or winter wheat on about 45 percent. Early and late crops of peanuts are harvested as well.

In Huadong, as elsewhere in China, there is both change and continuity. Even after half a century, returnees to the area might be struck with the similarity of the clothing and buildings of today to those of fifty years ago, the only notable difference being that now more brick construction is in evidence. Were such visitors to arrive during an early phase of spring or summer planting, they would see endless acres of flooded paddy fields, unaware perhaps that all the water is raised mechanically now rather than by human labor. They could still count many reliable water buffalo, though there is a hint of change in the number of small tractors at work. Lychee, melon, and *longan* ("dragon eye") orchards are visible beyond the paddy fields as well as fields of other crops —peanuts, soybeans, maize, rapeseed, and vegetables. The commune town appears extremely busy. Shoppers crowd the stores, and more customers are attracted by street vendors. The depth of political and social change in the area is most poignantly symbolized at the place where visitors are welcomed. What was once a Buddhist temple in the private compound of a prominent local clan now serves as the joint headquarters of the Huadong Commune Party Committee and the Huadong Commune Revolutionary Committee.

Older Huadong members recall that before the Communist period life in the area was hard, as it was in so many other rural communities in China. The former structure of power shows up in the local concentration of land ownership in those days: landlords and rich peasants—only 4 percent of the population—held 69 percent of the land. Suffering was a fact of life for many of the rest of the people, most of all for the lower-middle and poor peasants (together 84 percent of the population). County officials now estimate that only about 20 percent of the people back then had enough to eat all the time; 40 percent went hungry part of the time, and another 40 percent were always hungry. Their historical research indicates that for the two decades before the People's Republic, 6,840 Hua County peasants worked for landlords as hired hands in highly exploitative relationships; 4,400 migrated abroad; uncountable numbers drifted into Guangzhou to become beggars; 4,620 children were sold; 2,500 people were murdered; and 3,620 simply starved to death. Xiao Yingpiao, deputy chairman of Huadong Commune's Revolutionary Committee and deputy Party secretary, recounts what all this meant in personal terms.

> I was born in 1933 in what is now Chunying Brigade of Huashan Commune. This brigade borders on Huadong Commune to the west. Our family of seven was very poor. We owned three-quarters of an acre. I received six years of education. During the land reform classification, we were classified as "middle peasants." One year, 1943 or 1944, insect pests harmed so much of the crop that we had to eat wild vegetables. My mother died in childbirth that year due to weakness from hunger. My father tried to supplement our income by catching snakes in the hills. One day he was bitten by a snake and died because we could not afford a doctor. One younger sister died of smallpox, and my youngest sister died shortly after my mother died in childbirth because there was no one to nurse her. Out of our whole family, only my father's sister and I survived. She married and moved away. I managed to continue farming our land by exchanging labor with friends. In the first year of the new regime, at the end of 1950, I applied for a government job and was assigned to the Tax Bureau of Lianlong Xiang.[9]

These stark conditions were also reflected in the outbreak of a local rebellion. As early as 1927, one outraged peasant from Qiuhe Village, Wang Fushan, led a dozen or so others to study at the Peasant Movement Training Institute in Guangzhou City for six months. Upon their return home they organized peasant associations in several area villages. Their efforts culminated in a week-long armed struggle against a landlord-paid force at Pingshan. Their calls to arms were

"Down with Pingshan landlords," "Redistribute land and you'll have rice to cook," and "Down with local despots and bad gentry; freed peasants will be the masters." The Pingshan uprising was crushed and Wang was killed, but his comrades secretly carried on the struggle. Thus, long before the communists came down from the north, the area had its own revered tradition of popular revolt. During land reform in the early 1950s, several landlords in the area were executed.

Huadong, Tao Zhu, and Politics

Events of one period in Huadong's history, 1961-1965, clearly do set this commune apart. Tao Zhu, then first secretary of the powerful CCP Central-South Bureau (a regional Party organization covering the five provinces of Guangdong, Guangxi, Hunan, Hubei, and Henan), adopted Huadong Commune as a showcase during those years for controversial policies he favored. The central Party leadership was bitterly divided over agricultural policy after the Great Leap Forward. Some, like Chairman Mao, thought communes were basically a good idea and favored making only a few adjustments to correct obvious mistakes. Others, including Tao Zhu, thought that the only way to improve China's farm output was to abandon the collective organization of agriculture and to adopt a largely individual system that would reward farmers directly for their productivity. Leaders of Tao Zhu's persuasion at first favored "contracting production down to the household" (*bao chan dao hu*). But after Chairman Mao sharply criticized this proposal in September 1962 as a step toward the restoration of capitalism in the countryside, Tao and his allies called for a similar system known as the "paddy field management responsibility system of reward for production in excess of quota" ("responsibility system" for short). Its essence was captured in the slogan "three guarantees and one reward" (*san bao yi jiang*). This meant that individuals or families would take responsibility for a fixed plot of cropland and would guarantee the necessary labor to work it, a ceiling on the cost of working it, and minimum output from it. After harvesting, if actual output exceeded the quota guaranteed without a cost overrun, then those who had worked the land would receive 30 to 50 percent of the excess as a reward in kind or cash. On the other hand, if performance fell short of the guarantee, the 5 percent (apparently of the quota) would be charged as a penalty. Fertile plots were to be allotted to the highest bidders.

Why Tao Zhu chose Huadong as a showcase for these policies we do not know. One informant reports that as early as 1961-1962 Tao had singled out Huadong as a likely site for relocating factories from Guangzhou in the event of hostilities with Taiwan.[10] Another informant (a student from Guangzhou who had spent several weeks at Huadong on two different occasions) recalls that Tao Zhu proposed transferring two communes located within Guangzhou (Jiangcun and Dongfeng) to the jurisdiction of Hua County, thereby strengthening the economic base of his showcase county. Tao's plan was thwarted by determined opposition from farmers in Jiangcun and Dongfeng, which culminated in demonstrations that had to be quelled by soldiers. These farmers, the informant believes, were resisting the implied change in their tax liability and loss of their status allowing them to work legally in Guangzhou.[11] Whatever his reason for deciding on Huadong, Tao's intervention had a significant impact upon the commune's welfare.

Immediately after Tao returned from the Central Committee meeting where Mao had attacked contracting production down to the household, he and his Central-South Bureau colleagues "went deep" into twelve counties in Guangdong and Hunan. Huadong was one of their principal bases of operation.[12] When Tao first visited Huadong in October, he "favored Lixi Brigade with his distinguished presence" and there "confirmed the great power of the so-called responsi-

TABLE 1.2

Contributions Raised Under Central-South Bureau for Huadong as Keypoint

Level of Party Committee	Tao's Ordered Contributions ($)	Amount Actually Appropriated ($)
Central-South Bureau	200,000	75,000
Guangzhou Municipal Committee	75,000	50,000
County Committee	25,000	(25,000?)
Commune Committee	600,000	400,000
Total	900,000	550,000

Source: "Tao Zhu Is the Vanguard in Promoting Contracting Production Down to the Household--An Investigation into the Crime of Tao Zhu in Enforcing the Responsibility System of Rewards for Production in Excess of Quota at Huadong Commune," by 10,000 Li East Wind of Red Flag of Sun Yat-sen University under Red Headquarters of Guangzhou Combined Committee for Criticism of Tao Zhu, in Nanfang ribao (Southern Daily, Guangzhou), July 26, 1967, translated in Survey of China Mainland Press, No. 4011, (August 29, 1967), pp. 14-23.

bility system." On October 19, Tao convened a conference at Conghua, a town in the neighboring county, at which Huadong was designated a "keypoint" under the Central-South Bureau for promoting the responsibility system. As such, other communes in the region were to learn from Huadong.

During 1963, the responsibility system was extended to all of Huadong's twenty brigades. Huadong representatives were sent to publicize their experience at all relevant county, municipal, provincial, and regional conferences. Secretaries from nearby county and district (*zhuan qu*) Party committees were sent to Huadong "to receive the scriptures." Tao ordered all levels of Party committees under his jurisdiction to contribute substantial funds for his pilot scheme at Huadong, an order that met with impressive if not total compliance (see Table 1.2).

By 1964, many problems with the responsibility system had become evident. First, widespread corruption in at least one brigade had led Tao to single it out as a keypoint for the prosecution of the "four clean-ups campaign" (see note 10). Between June and December, he sent in twenty cadres from Guangzhou as a "work team" to run the campaign and personally visited the brigade twice during that period.[13] Second, a class bias appeared. Well-off farmers from the old days with experience cultivating their own land tended to prosper, while formerly poorer peasants who had mainly hired out their labor could not so easily make a go of it alone. A landlord family of eight in Lixi Brigade was able to earn $670 a year, not counting income from their private plot, $100 of which was cash reward. A poor peasant family of seven in the same brigade, by contrast, was fined $85 in 1963 owing to the failure of the *huang jiang* crop (a medicinal herb) they had undertaken to raise. As of 1965, this family was still not able to pay off its fine. Four persons of Shanxia Brigade, including one woman classified as landlord, together undertook to farm one-third of an acre of the paddy land of their own production team, guaranteeing an output of 138 kilograms of rice, in exchange for which they would be allotted 38 kilograms of chemical fertilizer and be given 570 workpoints. They actually harvested 410 kilograms. They were able to collect a large reward from the collective because their contracted quota was low. An upper-middle peasant household of Yangsheng Brigade undertook to farm about one-sixth of an acre of sugar cane, guaranteeing an output of 5,000 kilograms. They overfulfilled their contract by using only half the land for cane and made a profit of $150 selling vegetables grown on the other half. A local saying began to be heard, "Rewards bring smiles but fines bring tears." Most of the smiles, it seems, adorned the faces of people who had operated their own farms before the communist land reform. Third, significant amounts had to be paid from collective accounts as rewards. During the three years the responsibility system was in force in Shijiao Brigade, more than 60,000 kilograms of grain were paid out as reward

MAP 1.3
HUADONG PEOPLE'S COMMUNE
        TOPOGRAPHY

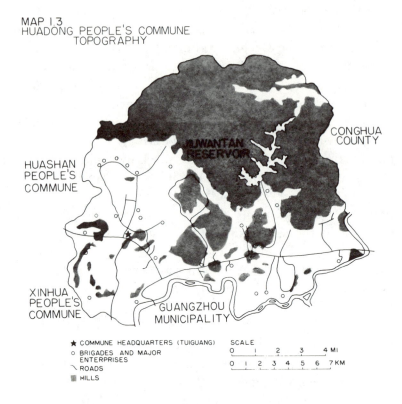

★ COMMUNE HEADQUARTERS (TUIGUANG)
○ BRIGADES AND MAJOR
    ENTERPRISES
⌐ ROADS
▓ HILLS

in kind. Yanghe Brigade's collective income from lychee alone fell by more than $50,000 in 1963, and a survey conducted in Lixi Brigade showed that many teams were paying out about 11 percent of their total income as rewards. Fourth, aggregate statistics on the standard of living showed a decline. In the period from 1962 to 1964, the number of poor teams (those with an average annual per capita income of $25 to $30) increased from 4 to 37, the number of hard-up households increased from 203 to 823, and the number of households with a deficit increased from 2,160 to 3,442. The overwhelming majority of these households were classified as poor or lower-middle peasant.

The gap between rich and poor grew wider as hard-up households paid fines while other families reaped rewards.

MAP I.4
HUADONG COMMUNE
RIVERS
AND
CANALS

~ RIVERS
≍ IRRIGATION CANALS

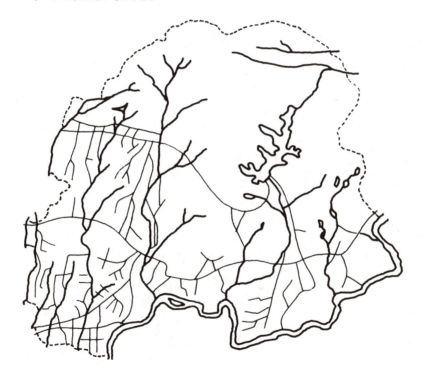

38

MAP I.5
HUADONG COMMUNE
HIGH-TENSION
 ELECTRIC
POWER GRID
 AND
WIRED BROADCAST
 NETWORK

ELECTRIC POWER GRID
WIRED BROADCAST
NETWORK

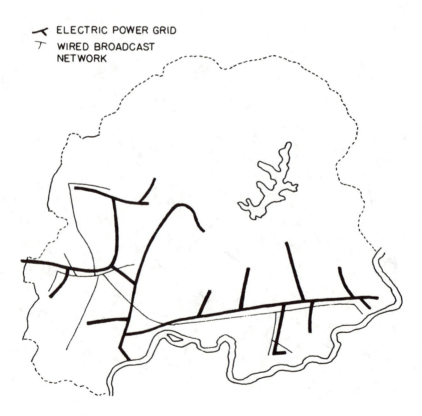

Finally, as a result of determined opposition from commune members, the responsibility system was abandoned in 1964. Tao Zhu himself was purged during the Cultural Revolution. In the late 1970s, Huadong Commune apparently holds no special status as a keypoint, but the legacies of Tao's attentions a decade before—investments in roads, waterworks, and chemical fertilizer—still contribute to its prosperity.

Huadong today, like China's 50,000 other communes, is vastly different from the bizarre creations of 1958. Our account of it is the story of one later, reorganized people's commune, tempered by the experience of the 1960s and 1970s.

Suggested Reading

Chu Li and Tien Chieh-yun, *Inside A People's Commune* (Peking: Foreign Languages Press, 1975).

Fei Hsiao-t'ung, *Peasant Life in China* (New York: Dutton, 1946).

Roy Hofheinz, Jr., "The Face of the Enemy: Hua County, 1926," chapter 9 in his *The Broken Wave* (Cambridge, Mass.: Harvard University Press, 1977), pp. 214-233.

Francis L. K. Hsu, *Under the Ancestor's Shadow: Kinship, Personality, and Social Mobility in China* (Stanford, Calif.: Stanford University Press, 1971).

Elizabeth Johnson and Graham Johnson, *Walking on Two Legs: Rural Development in South China* (Ottawa: International Development Research Center, 1976).

Peggy Printz and Paul Steinle, *Commune: Life in Rural China* (New York: Dodd, Mead, 1977).

Wu Chou, *Report from Tungting: A People's Commune on Taihu Lake* (Peking: Foreign Languages Press, 1975).

C. K. Yang, *A Chinese Village in Early Communist Transition* (Cambridge, Mass.: The M.I.T. Press, 1959).

2
Government and Politics

A frequently heard slogan in the People's Republic of China since the Cultural Revolution is *zhengzhi gua shuai*, "Put politics in command." This slogan describes a state of affairs that China's communist leaders would like to bring about, not necessarily one that exists already. The slogan is a call to action.

At the commune level, translation of central policies into action is the responsibility of a Party committee. This committee in turn directs the work of commune administrators under the day-to-day management of a hierarchy of revolutionary committees. Most prominent among all the Party's various leadership techniques is the mass campaign, an undertaking that attempts to combine effectively the potentially contradictory interests of Party will and of popular political participation. The contradiction can be dealt with and mass campaigns work well only if Party messages dominate all channels of communication and education, so that the leadership can saturate people's consciousness with official information and views. Formal law in these circumstances tends to sway before revolutionary priorities.

Chinese Communist Party

Huadong Commune has two leadership bodies, the Chinese Communist Party (CCP) and the Revolutionary Committee (RC). Together they exercise "dual leadership" over all that goes on in the commune. The Party is a national organization. It led the coalition of political forces that won the revolutionary struggle against the old Nationalist regime. According to its self-conception, the Party "represents" China's two most revolutionary classes, workers in the cities and poor and lower-middle peasants in the countryside. It chooses by its own criteria whom to accept as members, and it lays down its own policy directions. The Communist Party has organized a dominant coalition in China and exercises political leadership. It is "in power" in this sense. The local Party organization at Huadong is both a downward and an upward channel. It speaks authoritatively for the nationwide Party organization headquartered in Beijing and also reports its reading of local conditions in the commune up the line.

The Revolutionary Committee is the formally constituted "government" of Huadong Commune. It is elected every year by commune members. All decisions related to commune management must be approved by the RC, even though Huadong Party leaders might have made the decision beforehand and then applied their political power to secure the RC's agreement. The Party's power is evident in overlapping membership. Most of the RC's members (twenty-one out of twenty-five) are also Party members, including all eleven members of the RC's Standing Committee (six of whom also are members of the Party Committee's Standing Committee). The chairman of the RC, Xu Yunchen, doubles as secretary of the Party Committee.

The top level of the Party in the commune is the seven-member Standing Committee, which meets once a week. This leadership group is elected by and from among the twenty-one members of the Party Committee, which only meets about once every two months. All these individuals enjoy long tenure in office, even though they are elected every year or two by the commune Party congress. Generally speaking, Party members serving at this level are capable and respected people. The Huadong committeemen (and women) are returned to office again and again by the 450 delegates to the Party congress representing the 1,144 Party members in the whole commune. Some committee members develop specializations related to the economic life of the commune, such as in water conservancy, animal husbandry, or forestry. They may be sent to attend specialized courses, and after a while some of them come to be quite knowledgeable in their subject. Other Party committee members develop expertise in more strictly Party work, such as organization, membership and recruitment, propaganda and study, or women's affairs. They may attend training courses in a county or provincial Party school. Most of them hold positions in the commune administration (under the RC) and are responsible for day-to-day management of problems in their special area. As *Party* specialists, however, their job is to be concerned about broader matters of policy and political line.

Party structure in the commune parallels non-Party organization. The next level below the Party committee, the "Party branch," usually has between twenty and thirty members. Each branch meets about once a month and is responsible for Party work in its unit. Twenty branches are in production brigades, and twenty-two more are in commune administrative bureaus, enterprises, middle schools, the hospital, and the like. The basic level, called a "Party small group," exists wherever three or more Party members are found. Small groups meet once a week and afford the Party its most sensitive grass roots exposure. Many production teams have small groups along with shops, offices, clinics, primary schools, and pumping stations.

Roughly one Huadong Commune member in fifty-five (2 percent) belongs to the Party. The normal path to joining is for young men and women in the early teens to demonstrate a good attitude toward work and to stand out in political activities at school, thereby qualifying to join the Communist Youth League (generally in their late teens and early twenties). As Youth League members, if they show particular aptitude for ideological and political matters and take an active leadership role in League responsibilities, they may be recommended as probationary Party members. Should their progress continue as expected, they may be admitted as full members by their mid-twenties. An alternate path is first to join the People's Liberation Army. Political and technical training for soldiers is better than for civilians, and Party membership may be easier to attain there. Demobilized soldiers often return to their home village and expect to take an active role in local affairs. In the late 1960s, yet another path was through activism (on the winning side) in China's Great Proletarian Cultural Revolution. One main feature of the Cultural Revolution was Party rectification; Chairman Mao called for a mass movement to "expel the stale and take in the fresh," meaning to remove ineffective or incompetent Party members, replacing them with young activists who had proven themselves in the struggle. Fifty percent of the present Party membership of more than 35 million have joined since the Cultural Revolution; 20 percent have joined since 1973.

How do the people of Huadong feel about Party members? Lacking specific data about Huadong itself, we must rely here upon interviews with people from neighboring regions of Guangdong Province. In one view, the Party is an elite organization in which membership is highly desirable. Some people who hold this view may respect Party members they know personally and generally approve of the Party's leadership. Others may privately covet such elite status for private reasons—prestige, intrinsic interest of the work, enjoyment of power, income, security, advancement, or ability to attract a better marriage partner. In a second view, the Party's policies are too severe for the good they have brought. Although times are better now, life probably would have improved even without the Party's political rituals, intensive ideological study, and tiring mobilization for "great leaps." People who hold this view tend to regard Party members as arrogant and are regarded in turn by the Party as politically "backward." Some commune members expressed this sort of view in times of trouble, such as during the three years of bad weather and poor harvests (1959-1962) or during the Cultural Revolution, even though their outlook in more normal times is not so negative. A third view acknowledges the Party's success in equalizing living standards, economic security, and career opportunities but depreciates it because people no longer have a chance to improve their personal lot above the average. People who hold this view are essentially gamblers, preferring a society where fewer "make it" but where those few reap larger rewards. According to a fourth view, Party members are awarded too many privileges and garner automatic promotions even if they are no more competent than equivalent non-Party members in the same career line. Needless to say, some of these views are rooted in the social backgrounds of the people who express them. People who were exploited most viciously in the old society tend to appreciate their better chances today, whereas people who thought they could improve their lot under the old system are quicker to criticize the Party's more egalitarian approach today.

Revolutionary Committees and Administration

Although the commune and brigade Party committees monopolize political power and make all important decisions, the revolutionary committees (RCs) have a role of their own beyond simple implementation of Party policy. While the Party committees concern themselves only with selected priority matters, the RCs manage a full range of activities in the complex community and economy of Huadong.

Team members meet as often as two or three evenings a week to discuss the direction of their day-to-day affairs. Because team members live and work together, much discussion of issues and airing of opinion at this level occurs informally in the fields or at leisure. The most active participants are the team's "full labor power" members. They elect several of their number to hold positions of considerable responsibility. A team leader manages the team's various undertakings, often with the assistance of a deputy. A workpoint recorder keeps track of the value of each team member's labor and the number of hours per day he or she devotes to tasks of what difficulty rating. A warehouse keeper is responsible for the team's granary and stocks of other produce for storage or marketing. This same individual, in smaller teams, is also charged with seeing that the team's animals, machinery, and tools are cared for properly. Other responsible positions include political instructor, cashier, women's work leader, militia leader, and representative to the Poor and Lower-Middle Peasants' Association. In most teams, the real problem is to find people who are skillful enough, as well as sufficiently honest, reliable, and politically acceptable, to take on these jobs. It is not unusual for one capable individual to shoulder several tasks (the Chinese call such persons "10,000-talent cadres," *wan neng ganbu*) and to be reelected several times.

The team assembly sends seven or eight of its members to the brigade assembly, which in turn elects a revolutionary committee and leading brigade officials. At Huadong's Linong Brigade in 1971, four offices were up for election—leader, two deputy leaders, and accountant. One of the deputy leader positions was new. In the end, the three incumbents won reelection, as they had for all but one of the previous ten years, and a new person was added to the brigade leadership. Huadong spokesmen describe the nomination process as being very informal. Somehow, brigade members proposed seven candidates through discussion and recommendation. Five of the candidates, including all four who were elected, were Party members. Discussion continued, and by election day almost everyone's feelings were known. The secret ballot by the brigade assembly's 100 delegates resulted in a total of 360 votes for the four winners and 40 votes for the other three nominees. The brigade leader, Jiang Lihe, received 93 votes. Thus it seems that a shifting minority of roughly 10 percent cast votes against the winning slate. Since these jobs also require competent individuals, staffing them is a further drain on talent at the team level. A team's *wan neng ganbu* might be promoted.

Finally, brigade assemblies choose as many as fifteen or twenty delegates each as their representatives to the commune assembly. This body elects the Huadong Commune Revolutionary Committee. Because the commune serves as both the highest level of collective and the lowest level of local government, persons holding responsible jobs with the commune sometimes are recruited from outside Huadong. Xiao Yingpiao, for example, was born in a village of neighboring Huashan Commune. Before becoming deputy chairman of the Huadong RC, he was a cadre at the Lianlong *xiang* tax bureau.

Democratic impulses are strongest in the teams, while leadership impulses are strongest at the commune level, with the brigades falling between. In the relationship between brigades and teams, how much leadership and how much democracy are found depends upon the quality of a team's leadership and upon its economic success. Brigade leaders tend to concentrate their attention upon backward teams whose performance is poor; they are reluctant to interfere with successful teams. Huadong leaders cite three different ways to improve backward teams: (1) strengthen the leadership, (2) raise the level of political thought, and (3) give material assistance. While acknowledging that "objective conditions" (low soil fertility, difficult transportation) cannot be ignored, they believe that "subjective conditions" (morale, study, activism, leadership) are more important. If teams are burdened with "conservative" political thinking and have little faith in scientific farming, they are less able to organize

PLATE 5. Xiao Yingpiao. (Robert Neiderberger)

PLATE 6. *a*: Once a temple, this building now serves as Huadong Commune headquarters. (Robert Neiderberger) *b*: A brigade headquarters, complete with loudspeaker to transmit official broadcasts to villagers. (Andrew Nathan) *c*: A team workpoint recorder keeps track of the number of rows of rice seedlings that each worker transplants. His notched pole enables him to check at a glance whether the rows are the correct, agreed upon distance apart. (Andrew Nathan)

themselves to overcome objective barriers. Huadong spokesmen feel that it does little good simply to send in an outside
cadre to take over team leadership. Members themselves must
be taken to visit model teams and to study why the models
are more successful than their own team. If backward teams
show signs of improving subjectively, then commune funds
may be used to help out objectively. One promising
backward team at Huadong was given a tractor and had a
bridge constructed for them. The brigade may also intervene
in team affairs in connection with a current policy priority,
or when brigade leaders fear that they will be vulnerable to
charges of ideological laxity or even "rightism" if they ignore
a problem at the team level.

Nevertheless many teams still retain much control over
their affairs, even on such important matters as what crops to
plant and what work incentive practices to follow. In one
example, teams in a neighboring commune had been urged
late in the Cultural Revolution to distribute their collective
income after each harvest according to a mixture of two principles—need and work. Forty percent was distributed "according to need," that is, households with more people were given
a greater share regardless of how many workpoints they had
earned in contributing labor to the team. After a period of
trial, however, many teams decided that 40 percent "according to need" was too high, because the hardest workers were
not adequately rewarded for their effort. They voted to
reduce the amount distributed in this way to only 30
percent. A small number of teams even decided to do away
with distribution "according to need" altogether. Thus, by
the mid-1970s, some teams were distributing 60 percent of
their collective income "according to work"—that is, giving
proportionately greater shares to families who earned more
workpoints—while other teams were distributing 70 percent
according to the work principle, and a few more were distributing 100 percent in this way. Within the framework of
the state economic plan, which specifies minimum amounts

of grain production for each brigade, teams and brigades decide whether to produce more grain than required or to plant alternative crops. They also choose their own agricultural technology—how close to plant seeds, how much of what kinds of fertilizer to apply, when to transplant, and so on. They also decide what small enterprises to launch. Commune support for these decisions is needed only for equipment purchases and for the allocation of scarce commodities, such as chemical fertilizers.

The commune has a comparable relationship with higher authority. Some ideas are proposed to the commune as part of national or provincial plans. But if Huadong will be required to invest its own funds, its consent must be won. The decision rests with the commune RC under the unified leadership of the Huadong Party Committee. For example, one important problem arose at Huadong when the leadership became aware that they would soon face a shortage of electric power. According to Party policy, communes should be "self-reliant" (should not ask the state for funds unless absolutely necessary) and should "study Dazhai" (a model self-reliant brigade in North China). The Party committee asked the water conservancy and electricity group under the RC to conduct a preliminary study. This group was headed by a Party committee member and included an RC member, technicians, cadres, and peasants. It looked into the feasibility of constructing a new electric power generating station at Huadong, considering location, optimal size, design, cost, materials needed, allocation of manpower needed, and the need to enlist the cooperation of neighboring communes. They determined that a station could be built that would supply 50 percent of Huadong's foreseeable new power needs, but only at great cost. At this point, the Party organized a twenty-five-member delegation led by First Secretary Xu Yunchen and Deputy Secretary Xiao Yingpiao to travel to Dazhai Brigade in Shanxi Province to see for themselves the benefits of making the kind of sacrifices that

52

a

b

PLATE 7. *a*: "The Red Blossoms of Dazhai Bloom All Over" is the slogan in front of commune headquarters. (Robert Neiderberger) *b*: Peasant painting from Huxian, Shaanxi Province, extols class struggle themes. The banner in the center reads: "Workers, peasants, and soldiers are the main force in criticizing Lin Biao and Confucius." The lower

Dazhai had made. As a result of this widely discussed visit to the famous model brigade, arguments that Huadong ought to emulate Dazhai's advanced experience, practice "self-reliance" and "bitter struggle," and strive to "serve the people" and "reduce the burden of the state" carried more weight. After full discussion, the RC finally decided to go ahead with the investment. Powerful Party leadership and persuasion are evident in this decision process, but at no time was the Huadong Revolutionary Committee simply ordered to build a new power station.

Mass Movements

An important side of Huadong life about which, strangely enough, visitors have noted and written very little is "mass campaigns" (*yundong*). The oversight is strange because *yundong* are a key and highly visible element of Chinese communist leadership style and are emphasized heavily in Chinese articles. Every number of *Peking Review* reveals several move-

c

left slogan reads: "Never forget class struggle." The lower right slogan reads: "The philosophy of the Communist Party is a philosophy of struggle." *c*: Former landlord's residence in Huadong. The architecture of this structure is imposing, even by the standards of its day. (Charles Greer)

ments in progress—movements to "study Dazhai in agriculture," to "emulate Comrade Lei Feng" (a model soldier), to "criticize the 'gang of four,'" and to "struggle" against "class enemies" who wish to "restore capitalism" in China.[14] All these are carried on countrywide. Still more campaigns are conceived and run by local authorities alone. Catchwords are "study," "emulate," "criticize," and "struggle." *Yundong* in Chinese politics, like waves, come one after the other to mobilize popular participation behind the Party's priority public policy goals. The tasks of the many nationwide campaigns witnessed in China over the years have been defined relatively clearly, thus lending themselves to domination by cadres. An example was the movement to implement "open door schools" in which students were required to deal with work problems faced by nearby economic and scientific enterprises. The tasks of other campaigns have been defined more flexibly, thus leaving room for local variations and initiatives from below; participation in such campaigns has been more genuinely democratic. An example is the movement to "criticize Confucius," in which different localities identified their own manifestations of the evil influence of Confucian thinking.

People living and working in the teams of Huadong may learn about new campaigns in several ways—from broadcasts heard on the team loudspeaker, from occasional small group study sessions in the evenings at which newspaper articles about campaign tasks may be read and discussed, from political study meetings in the fields during work breaks, from team meetings, and from film and cultural performances. While mass movements are in progress, these activities typically intensify and may be supplemented by special campaign activities. Wall posters and banners carrying campaign slogans may appear, and some posters may go so far as to criticize by name persons whose behavior is considered by the poster writers to deviate from campaign ideals. As campaign events reach their crescendo, a brigade may organize public meetings to criticize or more intensively "struggle against" these deviant individuals in person, and perhaps to mete out some form of punishment.

The desire of most individuals to avoid strong public criticism or struggle brings an effective social control function to *yundong*. Cadres and ordinary peasants alike are vulnerable to campaign criticism. Hence, one effect of repetitive mass movements is to reduce the incidence of cadre corruption or misbehavior. Another effect is to check illegal activities by ordinary team members, such as shunning collective labor responsibilities in order to seek speculative private profits by buying, transporting, and selling scarce consumer goods to black market buyers.

A more positive *yundong* function is to mobilize the population for economic construction and other community purposes, such as public health and sanitation projects. Especially during the agricultural slack season, labor can be mobilized to clear new land, plant forests, or build water works. Other campaigns during the year mobilize people to carry out the most labor-intensive agricultural work—to transplant rice seedlings and to harvest, as well as to pay taxes on time, to repair farm implements, or to encourage mass participation in agricultural research.

The people of Huadong hold widely varying opinions on the subject of *yundong*. One extreme view is quite favorable —*yundong* effectively harness the joint power of the people who voluntarily work together for valuable community tasks that might never be performed if left to the state or to paid labor. The other extreme is very unfavorable—*yundong* are too hectic and political and override too easily the considered technical advice of skilled professionals: they trample on people's rights and can be economically destructive. But all the arguments for and against mass movements notwithstanding, they are firmly planted in the CCP's political leadership style, and they should continue to be a prominent feature of Huadong life for years to come.

Media and Political Communication

Channels of communication are tightly controlled in Huadong as they are elsewhere in China. People have access to only a relatively narrow range of officially approved information. This control plays an absolutely key role in China's revolutionary politics. According to Chinese ideology, the victorious working classes, led by the CCP, are still involved in a fierce class struggle with the overthrown exploiting classes who are trying to stage a comeback. Thus, the Party sees itself locked in combat with "class enemies" whose favorite tactic is spreading rumors and misinformation to deceive the people. Party leaders, to protect their revolutionary victory, feel that they must exercise "dictatorship of the proletariat" over all "counterrevolutionary" opposition. One weapon in this struggle is the communications media, the main instruments of political propaganda. The Party seeks to dominate China's printed and broadcast media alike with messages praising socialism, lauding the wisdom of the present leadership, and asserting endless optimism about the effectiveness of present policies. The Huadong RC has a deputy chairman for political education whose task is to manage work in this area. This deputy chairman presides over a hierarchy of people responsible for political education down to team-level political instructors. The Party, naturally enough, has a propaganda department to exercise overall leadership.

There is less organized political communication when no major mass campaign is in progress. Fewer team meetings are held, and attendance at even those meetings is lower. Villagers, especially the men, gather informally in the evenings to socialize, to talk over team affairs, and to discuss local politics. Many village women have similar opportunities while working together during the day. In this informal context, stripped of the rituals of more organized occasions, opinions may be expressed spontaneously and sincerely, especially among friends. Some of the more interesting information about events in other places and about goings-on at higher levels is passed along by word of mouth, known as "little broadcasts." This network seems to be taken quite seriously and enjoys relatively high credibility.

Huadong members who wish to become more adept at political study and to improve their political activism may attend their brigade's "political evening school for adults" three times each month. Other political meetings are called whenever the occasion demands—during festivals and holidays, on anniversaries of significant local achievements, or at the beginning of major undertakings at work such as plowing and planting.

Radio political messages are heard daily by almost everyone. Both Guangzhou Municipal People's Radio and Guangdong Provincial People's Radio broadcast from Guangzhou. Their transmissions are picked up in the commune headquarters by wireless receiver and relayed to a wired network of loudspeakers in brigade towns and teams. In the 1970s, most rural homes also have speakers (which can be turned on and off at will). Alternatively, teams, work groups, or individuals may decide to purchase their own transistorized radio receiver. Public speakers are found in train coaches and hotel rooms—in short, nearly everywhere. News reports and commentary on the air are often read from newspapers. Other programming includes music and drama, agricultural bulletins, and physical exercise routines. While some broadcasts use the official "national dialect" native to North China (which Westerners call "Mandarin"), many use "Cantonese," the local dialect.

China is a newcomer to the world of television. By the mid-1970s, China is estimated to have produced less than 500,000 black and white television sets, or an average of one set for about every 2,000 people. Television programs are transmitted a few hours each evening. Huadong residents can watch if their brigade has purchased a set and placed it in a

a

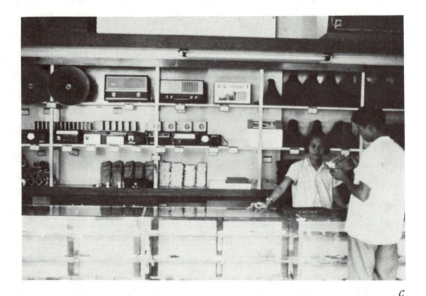

c

PLATE 8. *a*: Brigade-level teachers and a propaganda worker meet as a small study group. (Robert Neiderberger) *b*: Tuiguang branch of the Post and Telegraphic Office serves Huadong Commune. The "Newspaper Reading Board" (*yue bao lan*) to the left is crowned with two slogans: "Listen to what Chairman Mao says" and "Be concerned with important

b

d

state affairs." (Andrew Nathan) *c*: Households can purchase their own loudspeaker or radio receiver at this brigade store (may be Shaji Brigade south of Guangzhou). (Andrew Nathan) *d*: Team member inspects book display at commune department store. (Robert Neiderberger)

common room. Guangzhou City, thirty miles away, has one of only four or five stations in China equipped with studios that can originate live programs.

Visitors to Huadong are told that more than 75 percent of the commune population is "literate," though at what level is not clear. Ninety-five percent literacy is sometimes claimed for China as a whole, using a minimum standard of only 300 or 600 characters (higher middle school graduates recognize more than 3,500). For those residents of Huadong who do read newspapers, magazines, and books, political education is furthered through these media. Individuals rarely subscribe to periodicals, but some teams have them in small reading rooms and all brigades subscribe. Many commune members read newspapers displayed publicly on bulletin boards, page by page. These boards are found in town squares, at bus stops, and at village meeting places—wherever people linger and read them. In some cases, brigade school libraries open their doors for this purpose. The main national newspaper, the six-page *People's Daily,* is published in Guangzhou as well as in Beijing. The newspaper of the Guangdong Provincial Party Committee's Propaganda Department, the *Southern Daily,* is also received. It reprints lead stories from the *People's Daily* in addition to carrying its own stories about provincial affairs. Most of these stories concern ideological themes and criticism, accounts of successes by model units, and discussions of China's diplomatic stands and achievements. Capable political instructors in some teams have organized newspaper reading groups to discuss articles of local relevance. In other teams, such efforts have attracted little interest. In recent years, the *Reference News (Cankao xiaoxi),* which used to be internally distributed among high-ranking cadres, has been publicly posted in some brigade towns. The *Reference News* includes Chinese translations of news reports originally published in foreign journals such as *U.S. News and World Report,* the *London Times, Le Monde,* or the *Asahi Daily.* It provides readers with an additional window on the world outside.

The Huadong Supply and Marketing Coop general store and its branch stores in brigade towns all sell books. Team and brigade reading rooms and school libraries also purchase some books, and individuals can afford them. Most books are printed on low-grade paper, are bound with light paper covers, and are sold for reasonable prices (from just pennies to less than seventy-five cents). Titles include the published speeches of Mao Zedong, collections of articles on current political themes and criticism, stories and plays, and popular science editions on technical subjects ranging from radio repair to botany to earthquake prediction. Among people of more modest reading skills, illustrated "comic books" with political messages are popular.

When major mass campaigns are in progress, political communication intensifies. Conversations become more guarded as people share their inner thoughts only with dear and trusted friends. The content of all media—meetings, radio, newspapers and books—shifts to campaign themes. The number of meetings with political study agendas increases, they last longer, and attendance is higher. Some meetings may be held during working hours, and some of them may be held at the brigade town with correspondingly larger participation. Radio listening groups may be organized to hear a broadcast of an important national document. Another communications medium—the wall posters—may be pressed into use temporarily. "Big character posters" (*dazibao*) emblazon action slogans in prominent places, and "small character posters" contain virtual essays on campaign themes by individual or collective authors. These posters are handwritten with brush and ink on large sheets of paper handily provided by the Supply and Marketing Coop. People read and discuss the poster articles, and some may decide to pen a poster of their own, taking issue with one already displayed. Thus, during mass campaigns, debates by poster are added to the regular channels of political communication.

a

b

PLATE 9. *a*: Huadong station of the Hua County Public Security Bureau. (Andrew Nathan) *b*: Painting and slogan in front of commune headquarters call for the whole country to study the People's Liberation Army, and for the PLA to learn from the people. (Robert Neiderberger) *c*: Hua County people's court at Tuiguang. (Andrew Nathan)

花县推广人民法庭

c

Law and Public Security Forces

The idea of law has high stature in Western Europe and America because it embodies the ideal of limited government. Citizens are guaranteed civil rights, and people care as much about due process as they do about the substance of legal decisions. Important matters, notably religious convictions and ethical preferences, are generally considered to lie outside the legitimate domain of governmental interference, and hence beyond the reach of law. Recently, for example, the United States Supreme Court (in *Miller* v. *California*, 1973) shrank from the task of setting a uniform standard for obscenity, preferring instead to leave individual communities wide scope in setting their own standards. In the Western ideal, justice is blind to power, wealth, and social position. She hears only properly admitted evidence and impartially decides each case on its merits.

In Chinese civilization, however, the ideal of limited government has never caught on. The old emperor was all-powerful outside the realm of local affairs, and the modern socialist regime is proclaimed as a "dictatorship of the proletariat." Religion and ethics have never been considered private and beyond governmental authority. The substance of public decisions has always been treated as more important than the decision process. Chinese philosophers have concerned themselves less with big government than with bad government. The rule of virtue, or of virtuous men, is prized above the entangling rule of law.

The value of direct community concern for deviance is found in both traditional and modern Chinese culture. The West's insistence upon individual freedom and privacy leads in the opposite direction; potentially deviant persons generally are left alone until they are suspected of clearly committing a crime, at which point law enforcement machinery is activated against them. Accused persons must hire counsel to represent them throughout the complex and often incomprehensible legal proceedings that follow. But short of actual criminal conduct, no one meddles in their affairs. China works differently. Standards of conduct are widely publicized in newspapers and other propaganda media, often in the guise of stories about model persons or groups. Everyone discusses these stories in regular political study groups. Passivity in political study, as much as open expression of deviant attitudes, alerts fellow group members to persons with "problems." Group pressure in the form of persuasion, criticism, or punishment of some sort is tried before the problem is turned over to any authority. Such activity intensifies during mass campaigns. The law in China is a last resort, not a first response.

All this may help to explain why China has less than 10,000 law school graduates, at most about 2 percent of the number in the United States. Even judges are not required to have formal legal training. To enforce the law when necessary, China has a national police force administered under the Ministry of Public Security. By all reports, this force has not grown into a Stalinist sort of secret police. Rather, its role has been very subdued, probably because other forms of social control have worked so effectively. The Public Security Bureau nearest to Huadong is a Huaxian, the county seat. The commune has only one officer posted to a modest branch police station (*paichusuo*), and he functions more as a communications link than as a ready instrument of police power. Huadong's own public security apparatus takes the form of "order preservation committees" at the commune and brigade levels. These committees recruit personnel as needed among militia members and others and are empowered to arrest and detain, to investigate, and to impose and administer limited penalties.

China has formal laws—a marriage law, a labor code, commercial regulations, and others—which are published and thoroughly disseminated through small group study. Most of them are not elaborate, however. They are more like descriptions of the spirit of the law, or expressions of legislative intent. Legal proceedings never involve fine points or technicalities, since only rough guidelines are written down. One effect is to give great latitude of discretion to local public security cadres and judges; another is to allow the legal system to be very responsive to local political demands. The Chinese Communists have been extremely reluctant to codify laws and to establish a legal profession except where absolutely necessary (for example, in the field of foreign trade) for fear of limiting their revolutionary political authority in undesirable ways. Nevertheless, many Chinese favor more extensive codification. In years to come, this will probably occur gradually.

Huadong's least serious civil disputes stem from marital problems or complaints by one neighbor against another (for example, Li complains that Zhang's pig has trampled his garden). For civil matters like these, teams have a "people's mediation committee" of three to five members. The committee meets after work whenever the parties to a dispute voluntarily agree to put their cases before the neutral authority. People's mediation committees are also found at the brigade and commune levels, where they deal with similar civil disputes between teams or between individuals and enterprises, or listen to cases that a team mediation committee cannot resolve (perhaps because feuding families are involved).

Individuals who remain unsatisfied with the results of neighborly mediation may initiate a civil suit before the county People's Court, but this course of action is discouraged and people follow it only rarely. A small courthouse is located at Tuiguang near commune headquarters. No lawyers are hired. A judge alone listens to all arguments (and perhaps consults with local leadership in the litigants' area), then decides the issue on the basis of law and equity (and perhaps politics).

Disputes with more serious political overtones normally are handled by a brigade Party branch or by the commune Party Committee. For example, if a downstream team feels that an upstream team is taking too much water from their common waterway, then brigade Party leaders would certainly intervene to preserve harmony among the teams.

Much petty criminal behavior is handled outside the courts. Whether team or brigade members act directly against a wrongdoer, or whether they hand the problem over to public security cadres, in part depends upon how closely their personal interests are touched. On the one hand, individuals who steal from a team warehouse or burglarize homes normally are brought before a team meeting (or perhaps a brigade meeting in more serious cases, including multiple offenses) and are required to write a self-criticism for public posting in prominent places or to deliver personally a humiliating self-criticism at a public meeting. Sometimes the offender is physically beaten at these meetings by outraged neighbors and team or brigade members. Often the accused's first effort at self-criticism is not accepted by the group, and several more thorough and "sincere" ones are demanded. These meetings may last for hours. Individuals who offend the team's moral standards by gambling excessively or by having an illicit love affair are also exposed to direct public action of this sort. On the other hand, a crime that does not directly victimize team members is more likely to be referred to brigade public security authorities. Crimes of this nature include illegal speculation in commodities or attempted illegal emigration to Hongkong. Huadong's public security authorities, acting on their own, may decide to post offenders' photographs around the commune and warn people not to buy from or sell to them. Or they may parade offenders through all the brigade towns one by one, to be publicly displayed as negative examples.

A special case arises when the wrongdoer happens to be a cadre, perhaps even a Party member. The situation is not uncommon, since cadres can be powerful persons in their own locality, and they have ample opportunities to enrich themselves from the team or brigade or to demand sexual favors. If a corrupt cadre is the most capable leader available, however, people may tolerate corruption up to a point if they fear that removing the erring cadre from office might cause their incomes to decline. One emigré reported a case of this type at a commune not far from Huadong. It was discovered that a man doubling as team leader and team warehouse keeper (in itself suggesting the lack of qualified people to assume management responsibilities) had pilfered a basket of peanuts from the team's warehouse to sell privately. The team member who made the discovery and reported the crime brought the evidence to the brigade's Order Preservation Committee. This committee in turn called for the team to meet to hear the leader's self-criticism. When this meeting was held, the leader admitted his greed and promised to compensate his team for the losses he had caused. A brigade cadre representing the Order Preservation Committee concluded the meeting by announcing that the man no longer could be warehouse keeper but could remain as team leader. Angry team members demanded the fellow's dismissal as leader as well, whereupon several brigade cadres visited members of the team to persuade them that, since their leader had expressed repentence, he should be given a second chance. Overall, they argued, he had been an effective team leader. They succeeded in keeping him on.

Serious crimes—including substantial or repeated theft, violent acts such as rape or murder, or overt acts of opposition to communist rule—are handled by the Hua County Public Security Bureau. Depending on the circumstances, the bureau may rely on Huadong's own security personnel, or they may dispatch police from the county seat. Intervention by the bureau may result in harsher sanctions. The least of these, termed "current supervision," is analogous to a severe form of parole. A specific period is set for supervision, say three years. During this period "elements currently under supervision" (*bei xian guan fenzi*) may be denied the right to communicate by mail with people outside Huadong; they are deprived of their civil rights (*bei chiduo gongmin quan*); and in general they are not considered to be regular team members. One emigré from a nearby commune who had experienced this sanction recalls, "It was like being in prison but without the prison." The next step up, "labor education" (*lao jiao*), takes individuals away from their home team for a period of months to go through a more rigidly supervised regimen of hard labor and writing of self-criticisms. The next step up after that, "labor reform" (*lao gai*), sends wrongdoers to a labor camp where conditions resemble a prison farm or mine for a year or more. In a tiny number of severe cases, prison terms and even executions are meted out. All serious offenders are handled by the county People's Court at Huaxian, not by the local court at Tuiguang.

Mention must be made of China's political criminals—"landlords, rich peasants, counterrevolutionaries, rightists, and bad elements" in the Chinese idiom. At Huadong as elsewhere, these "five black elements" account for about 5 percent of the population. They are people who supported the old regime the communist revolution overthrew, or who exemplify in their present behavior the CCP's characterization of the old society and its evils. As such, they are labeled "enemies of the people" and lead lives totally without opportunity. They are criticized routinely during mass campaigns. They may not hold leading cadre positions. Their children are denied advancement to higher education or to Party membership. In some teams where revolutionary politics run strong, other team members do not take the "five elements" as friends and even refuse to talk to them. Many of these labeled elements despair that their families will ever be able to lead normal lives in revolutionary China, and some attempt to flee to Hongkong or Macao. There, despite all uncertainties, at least people of their social station are not treated automatically as political outcasts.

Finally, Huadong Commune's militia members number almost 8,000, of whom 43 percent are women. They train to support the regular army in wartime; they help with non-routine tasks such as fire fighting and land reclamation; and they perform occasional police services such as guarding ripe crops against thieves. In wartime, they would function as both producers and fighters. Militia leaders typically are veteran army officers. They organize training exercises with a nearby unit of the People's Liberation Army during periods when agricultural work is slack. (Soldiers from a PLA unit near Huadong also give instruction in small arms and guerrilla tactics. On one occasion, a group of them took up residence on the commune for six months.) The brigade-level unit of the militia is a company. Ten of these companies are recognized as "four-good" (i.e., good in political thought, work style, military training, and management of living). Linong Brigade has 380 militia members, ranging in age from sixteen to twenty-five. Rifles used by brigade militia companies are stored at the commune between training exercises, with the exception of five to ten that are always kept in each brigade. The militia platoon is found at the team level. At this level at Huadong, 5,600 individuals are distinguished as "four-good" militia members.

In contrast to the imperial system of old, modern Communist Party organization plunges deep into local society. Party leaders want broad masses of people, not just elites, to be on their side, a goal they recognize as ambitious, but toward which they persevere out of a firm belief in its righteousness.

Suggested Reading

Chinese Communist Party

Richard Baum, *Prelude to Revolution: Mao, the Party and the Peasant Question* (New York: Columbia University Press, 1975).

Parris H. Chang, *Power and Policy in China* (University Park: Pennsylvania State University Press, 1975).

John Wilson Lewis, *Leadership in Communist China* (Ithaca, N.Y.: Cornell University Press, 1963).

John Wilson Lewis, ed., *Party Leadership and Revolutionary Power in China* (Cambridge, England: Cambridge University Press, 1970).

Revolutionary Committees and Administration

A. Doak Barnett, *Cadres, Bureaucracy, and Political Power in Communist China* (New York: Columbia University Press, 1967).

Jack Chen, *A Year in Upper Felicity: Life in a Chinese Village during the Cultural Revolution* (New York: Macmillan, 1973).

Jan Myrdal, *Report from a Chinese Village* (New York: Pantheon, 1965).

Franz Schurmann, *Ideology and Organization in Communist*

China (Berkeley and Los Angeles: University of California Press, 1968).

Mass Movements

Gordon Bennett, *Yundong: Mass Campaigns in Chinese Communist Leadership* (Berkeley: Center for Chinese Studies, University of California Press, 1976).

Charles P. Cell, *Revolution at Work: Mobilization Campaigns in China* (New York: Academic Press, 1977).

Media and Political Communication

Alan P. Liu, *Communications and Political Integration in Communist China* (Berkeley and Los Angeles: University of California Press, 1971).

Frederick T. C. Yu, *Mass Persuasion in Communist China* (New York: Praeger, 1964).

Law and Public Security Forces

Victor H. Li, *Law Without Lawyers: A Comparative View of Law in the United States and China* (Boulder, Colo.: Westview Press, 1978).

Martin King Whyte, *Small Groups and Political Rituals in China* (Berkeley and Los Angeles: University of California Press, 1974).

Amy Auerbacher Wilson, Sidney Leonard Greenblatt, and Richard Whittingham Wilson, eds., *Deviance and Social Control in Chinese Society* (New York: Praeger, 1977).

3
Economy

Chairman Mao's most famous instruction on economic policy was *fazhan jingji, baozhang gongji:* "Develop the economy and insure supplies." In it, he alluded to the universal contradiction between growth and consumption—enjoying later or enjoying now. Mao's message was that neither one should be slighted in the Party's policies.

In agriculture the "key link" is said to be grain (which includes rice). Yet the southern Chinese farm economy thrives on much more than rice. Rural prosperity also depends upon small-scale industries run by brigades, communes, and counties, and upon uncountable private undertakings of individual households. Agricultural markets, consequently, are partly public and partly private. A most interesting issue has been arrangement of work incentives on farms, that is, whether to reward individual productivity, or whether to emphasize the accomplishments of collective production. A stalemate between the competing logics supporting these choices has necessarily led to compromises between the opposing policies. Commune members' living standards directly reflect this contradiction. Most individuals are better off now than they were a generation ago, but their personal consumption levels are now more nearly equal than before.

Grain Farming

Huadong's fields, straddling the Tropic of Cancer, are at the same latitude as Dacca, Bangladesh, Egypt's Aswan Dam, Havana, and Honolulu. Overall the climate is tropical—hot and wet, allowing an eleven-month growing season. Annual temperatures range from the high fifties to the mid-eighties, except for the northern hills which may experience frost in January and February. Annual rainfall normally exceeds sixty inches. November through February are relatively dry months, averaging one and a quarter inches of rainfall per month. April through September are wet months, averaging more than eight inches per month. The "South China rainy season" during May and early June brings over ten inches per month. According to a local saying from the old days, "Summer flood waters are wide and deep, but in winter we flee drought." Huadong falls within an area of South China that is unusually favorable to agriculture. An early wet rice crop (four-month growing season) is harvested in late June or early July. A late wet rice crop (four-month growing season) is harvested between mid-October and mid-November. A third "catch crop" of barley or winter wheat (three-month growing season) is harvested about February. The sandy soil with an admixture of clay is not highly fertile. Wet rice agriculture, however, depends less upon the soil's fertility than upon its water retentiveness. Summarized sketchily, improvements in rice yields at Huadong are given to visitors as in the table at the top of the next page. The 1973 Huadong figure compares favorably with the target of nearly 2.25 metric tons of rice per acre set for areas south of the Yangzi River in China's National Agricultural Development Plan (formally ratified in April 1960). Further impressive gains may be more difficult to realize, because most of the easiest farm improvements already have been made. Application of chemical fertilizer, however, is still well below the amount that could be economically absorbed.

Period	Metric tons/acre	Jin/mou*
1940s (average while China was at war)	0.9	300
1957 (after consolidation of the new regime)	1.4	450
1958 (after one year of Great Leap Forward water con-servancy construction)	1.8	600
1973	3.0	1,000
1976	3.4	1,137

*A *jin* (*chin*, catty) = 0.5 kilogram. A *mou* = 0.17 acre.

Rice farming at Huadong is still labor-intensive, although this is changing slowly. First the fields are plowed, then compost (from animal and green manure) is added, balks (mud ridges separating fields) are repaired, and seed beds are sown. Next, after the rains come and the fields are water-logged, heavy wooden rakes are dragged backwards and for-wards by water buffalo or by light tractor or cultivator until the whole surface reaches the consistency of thick potato soup. Now the field is ready for transplanting. Bundles of seedlings are pulled up from the seed beds and planted, either laboriously by hand or (increasingly now) with the help of mechanical transplanters in remarkably regular lines in stands of four to five seedlings together. It was once the accepted wisdom that the field should be kept wet from transplanting until shortly before harvesting, preferably under a constant cover of four to five inches of water. As an added benefit, the field could be used simultaneously for raising fish, and the fish would keep the water free of mosquito larvae. A new technique gaining popularity since the 1950s, however, is to divide the growth of late rice into three stages—"tillering," "booting," and "heading." At the end of each stage, the growth of stems and leaves is checked by draining off the water and letting the field dry. This prevents top-heavy plants from falling down by stimulating the growth of roots. By

a

c

PLATE 10. *a*: A walking tractor plows five acres per day, compared with a water buffalo's one-half acre per day. (Andrew Nathan) *b*: The buffalo's advantages are maneuverability in delicately balked paddy fields, and production of two tons of organic fertilizer per year. (Robert

b

d

Neiderberger) *c* and *d*: Team field workers transplant young rice seedlings in newly plowed and flooded fields. The time is late July, toward
the beginning of the second growing season. (Andrew Nathan)

either approach, available chemical fertilizer is broadcast at appropriate times for maximum effect. To secure a good crop, the field must be weeded two or three times before harvest. Reaping is then done by hand, usually by means of toothed sickles. Threshing used to be done in the field by beating the heads of grain over the edge of a screened tub, or by using pedal-operated threshers. Most production teams have now invested in threshing machines. Demand for farm labor peaks at transplanting and harvesting times when even youth from Guangzhou and soldiers from nearby bases may be mobilized to help.

Central to this process is water control. Seasonally concentrated rains and the flood prone Liuqi River must be translated by an intricate system of progressively smaller irrigation canals into a stable four- to five-inch water cover over 10,000 acres (sixteen square miles) of delicately balked rice paddies. Two of Huadong's biggest annual campaigns to mobilize labor for water conservancy construction occurred immediately after the commune's founding in 1959 and 1960, as if to demonstrate that commune organization was a superior administrative vehicle for building necessary waterworks. Subsequent campaigns of note were organized in 1964 and 1969. All construction campaigns are carried out during the agricultural slack season, which at Huadong occurs from November through January. Only about 40 percent of the cultivated acreage is farmed during that season, the prevailing weather is warm and dry with clear skies, and water levels are low—ideal, one might say, for strenuous outdoor labor. During these four campaigns, Huadong and a half a dozen neighboring communes constructed fifty-six miles of canals, eleven miles of dikes, two barrages in the Liuqi River, twenty-six reservoirs and ponds in the highlands, two hydroelectric generating plants, a grid of high-tension transmission lines, and four electrically powered pumping stations in flood prone areas. Huadong itself mobilized 8,000 workers to dig fifteen miles of the seventy-five mile "New Liuqi" Canal.

This canal and other waterworks have brought 96 percent of Huadong's fields under gravity-feed irrigation, and electrically powered pumps raise the other 4 percent. Before the formation of the commune, this survival task of raising and maintaining the water level required an enormous expenditure of physical labor. With these improvements, approximately half the labor force has been relieved of water raising and carrying duties to pursue other production tasks.

Some changes do not come easily. Any modernization of traditional farming methods that fit social and geographical realities and have earned a certain reputation for rationality and efficiency raises practical problems that cannot be ignored. First, while water mechanization has been welcome, other mechanization has entailed problems. Tractors are less able than water buffalo to preserve delicately balked paddy fields or to cultivate vegetable plots nestled between rows of orchard or forest trees. Walking tractors have been developed which are almost as good, but they require gasoline and give no manure. Only as China's petroleum industry develops to a point where low-cost gasoline and inexpensive chemical fertilizers are available will these disadvantages decline in importance. Moreover, peasants who earn their livelihoods from labor-intensive agriculture fear unemployment due to agricultural mechanization. Many such fears of unemployment are exaggerated. Labor in China can be reassigned easily to rural small industries or construction. Unemployment effects depend on the type of mechanization: insecticides may eliminate the need for weeding, but a new pump may allow a whole new crop cycle. Second, closer planting necessitates greater fertilizer application. Chemical fertilizer must be locally manufactured from petrochemicals (by one unsubstantiated report, two small plants for this purpose were built at Huadong in 1964), or it must be purchased. Skill in applying it properly must also be developed. Third, deeper plowing necessitates more power (a buffalo can pull only a traditional three- to four-inch blade). The added power must come from tractors, which require not only fuel but also drivers and mechanics. Finally, deeper plowing runs the risk of disturbing the iron pan, an impervious layer needed to prevent water seepage that heavier and less porous South China soils tend to develop eighteen to twenty-four inches under the surface. The point is that many facets of rural production and life are interrelated. Planned change of one facet may bring unintended consequences, and it cannot be accomplished overnight.

Rice cultivation essentially is a production team activity which brigades and the commune support. Assistance in the form of political leadership, large waterworks construction, electrification, commercial services, and large machinery supply and maintenance is covered elsewhere. Here we need only highlight one other form—demonstration and research. To convince skeptical team members to adopt innovations—tractors, cultivators, transplanters, short stalk (typhoon resistant) high-yield rice, chemical fertilizer, insecticides, deep plowing, close planting, substituting winter wheat for barley, and so on—the commune maintains some 1,100 acres of "demonstration plots" throughout its territory (9 percent of the total cultivated area). Huadong's farmers know that these plots receive special attention and that their impressively higher yields may not be easy to duplicate on ordinary plots. Nevertheless, significant persuasion and training are achieved with the help of the demonstration fields. In the case of nitrogenous fertilizers such as ammonium sulphate, for example, improper use results in bizarre consequences. Unlike compost, which enriches soil for an entire growing season, chemical fertilizer gives only brief and very intense enrichment. Applying it at the wrong time or at the wrong depth may easily stimulate long stems and oversized leaves but have no positive effect on grain production. Putting an innovation into practice on highly visible demonstration plots allows team members to observe fully a new technique first hand.

Research is needed to discover which of many available new agricultural technologies are most suited to the specific soil and climatic conditions of Huadong. The commune formed an Agricultural Research Center in its second year to undertake seed breeding, experimentation with new crops, agronomic experimentation (e.g., optimal application of water and insecticides), maintenance of weather records, and management of the demonstration plots. The Center employed twenty-seven technical workers in 1973, and ten acres were set aside for its work. At the brigade level, a total of fifty-one technical workers (two or three per brigade) were employed then at agricultural research stations; altogether they maintained thirteen additional acres of experimental and seed breeding plots.

James Nickum, drawing heavily upon notes taken by Richard Shen, has given a more technical account of wet rice farming at Huadong. Both were members of a hydrology and water management delegation that visited Huadong in 1974.

> The water management technique for growing rice is as follows: when planting the sprout, use 3 cm. of water; it then recovers to green color in 15 days. From the 15th day to between the 30th and 35th days, maintain shallow water (in which one can see the mud surface) to hasten division. From 35th to 40th day expose the field to the sun's heat in order to develop strong roots. From days 40-45, give 5 days baking, then add water but drain on the 50th day. As the grains form, maintain shallow water. In the last ten or more days, keep it damp until the grains ripen and turn yellow. Thus the formula is: wet green and dry yellow, alternating three times; it is ready for harvest in the final dry yellow days. Fifteen days after transplanting until the 30th day, weed. There are three harvests a year; the first two average 512 catties/*mou*, the last 508. Maximum yields exceed 1,000 catties/*mou*, while low yield fields may reap 300-400.
>
> On double-crop fields, 1,200-1,500 kilograms of green fertilizer and 900 kg. of organic fertilizer are used per *mou*. In 1973, 23 kg. of ammonia and 45 kg. of phosphate were used on each *mou* for the three crops. Water is applied at the rate of

140 cubic meters per crop per *mou,* although this naturally depends on the amount of precipitation.[15]

Enterprises, Sidelines, and Private Plots

We have analyzed grain farming in some detail, both because rice is Huadong's single most important crop and because products of the grain harvest are four-fifths of the average person's diet at Huadong. Other economic activities are extremely important too, however, as a glance at Table 3.1 will show. Production teams earn almost as much income from their nongrain crops and other sidelines as they do from grain farming (see columns 1 and 2). Private undertakings of households add about 25 percent to the income they receive from their team (see columns 3 and 7). Households generate nearly as much income as commune-level small industrial enterprises, and twice as much as brigade-level enterprises (see column 8). What is more, however, these small-scale enterprises serve an important purpose other than generating income. They help make Huadong "self-reliant" by supplying locally produced goods for farming and a variety of consumer goods for households.

Small-scale industries. The scale of investment in manufacturing depends upon the size of the unit making the investment. Brigades establish tiny factories, communes found small ones, and state administrative divisions or ministries act as entrepreneurs for large factories. At Huadong, for example, brigades operate five small peanut oil pressing mills, while the commune operates two bigger ones. Twelve small coal mines are brigade enterprises, but the biggest one is a commune enterprise. As of 1973, the commune operated fifteen small-scale industries employing fewer than 900 workers and brigades operated another forty-five employing an unknown number. Thus, of a total work force of 28,000 (85 percent of them full-time), the proportion working in this sector was still quite modest, though it is likely to increase

TABLE 3.1

Estimated Income of Huadong People's Commune, 1972 (in thousands of $US)

Level	(1) Collective income from grain farming	(2) Collective income from subsidiary agriculture and sideline undertakings	(3) Distribution to members	(4) Collective income from small industrial enterprises	(5) Enterprise profit	(6) Total collective income (1+2+4) Amt.	%	(7) Household income from sideline undertakings and private plots	(8) Total income, collective and household (6+7) Amt.	%
Households								784	784	10
Teams	3075	2515	2740			5590	81		5590	73
Brigades				403	108	403	6		403	5
Commune				937	169	937	13		937	12
Total	3075	2515	2740	1340	277	6930	100	784	7714	100
Percent	40	33		17		90		10	100	

Source: Adapted from Claude Aubert, "People's Communes—How to Use the Standard Visit," New Left Review, No. 89 (January-February 1975) pp. 86-96, and Ward Morehouse, "Notes on Hua-tung Commune," China Quarterly, No. 67 (September 1976), pp. 582-596.

a

b

e

f

PLATE 11. *a*: Hydroelectric power generator. (Robert Neiderberger)
b: One of Huadong's thirteen small coal mines. (Robert Neiderberger)
c, d, and *e*: At this kiln, which manufactures both piping and ceramic
ware for household use, heat produced at the lowest level efficiently
fires pottery at each higher "step." (Robert Neiderberger) *f*: Lathe

c

d

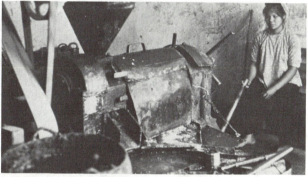

g

h

operator in one of the commune machine shops. (Robert Neiderberger) g: Press for extracting oil from peanuts. (Robert Neiderberger) h: This machine roasts peanuts while stirring them slowly. The roasting fire is fueled with peanut shells. (Robert Neiderberger)

a

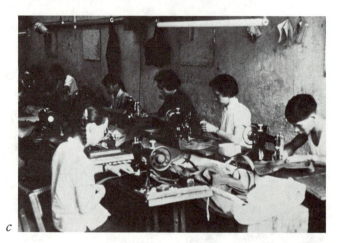

c

PLATE 12. *a*: Workers assemble a thresher in the farm implement factory. (Andrew Nathan) *b*: Most completed threshers are sold to nearby communes. The cadre pictured is Xiao Yingpiao. (Robert Neiderberger) *c*: Men and women brigade members make small canvas bags. (Robert Neiderberger) *d*: Making pearls. One girl cuts tiny strips of oyster flesh to use as irritants. The other girl makes tiny incisions in membranes of oyster tissue, and implants the irritants. (Robert Neiderberger) *e*: Zhang Liyi in front of his family's private plot. See pp. 108-113 for more detail on the Zhang family. (Andrew Nathan)

b

d

e

in future years. Some commune factories began production to meet Huadong's own needs and then later sought outside orders. In 1973, for example, the farm implements factory sold only 10 of its threshers to Huadong teams, which were fairly well equipped already, and 490 to outside teams. That same year, the coal mines collectively sold 5,600 tons of coal in Huadong and marketed 15,600 tons in Guangzhou. These enterprises probably pay taxes to the state, but net profits are retained by the collective units that operate them. Roughly 60 percent of these profits is invested in agriculture, 30 percent is reinvested in industrial undertakings, and 10 percent is deposited in social welfare funds (see columns 4 and 5 of Table 3.1).

Electric power for local factories is a by-product of water conservancy projects. A dam built for irrigation control can include a hydroelectric power station. By 1973, Huadong's power stations generated about 55 percent of its electricity. For agricultural use, apparently, power is sold at close to cost (two cents per kilowatt hour). A slight profit is taken on sales to factories, and households pay about twice the cost.[16]

Collective sideline undertakings. Sidelines are agricultural or other economic activities above and beyond a team's principal responsibility, which at Huadong is grain production. Sidelines can be nonstaple food products like pigs, fish, ducks, vegetables, or fruit. They can be strictly "economic crops" such as herbs needed as ingredients in Chinese medicines, or they can be cottage industries or services such as sandal making or tailoring. Most sidelines are carried on by individual households; only occasionally is a group or a machine required. Some teams simply prefer to undertake a profitable activity collectively to maximize team income or stifle incipient "capitalism" among enterprising families (or both). Other teams regard this as a progressive step and collectivize all important sidelines, pig raising in particular. Still other teams leave the whole sector to family enterprises.

Household sideline undertakings. This lively sector, as revealed in column 7 of Table 3.1, accounted for $784,000 in sales in 1972. This amounts to one-tenth of all income earned in the commune that year. Such sidelines are important in the national economy, too. In 1973, one-fourth of all agricultural and sideline products purchased by state commercial departments were products of household sideline occupations, such as hogs, domestic fowl, fresh eggs, rabbits, wild fibers, and wild medicinal herbs.[17] During the Great Leap Forward, zealous communists had wanted to eliminate the private sector altogether. Later, however, the anger of families who were denied the extra income, coupled with the anger of people in general who were annoyed by shortages of almost every category of consumer good, led Party leaders away from this policy. A proposal to "contract production down to the household" was even advanced at one point (see the section about Tao Zhu in the Introduction), but there Party leaders drew the line. Nowadays households either sell their products on local markets within controlled price ranges, or they sell them to a commercial agency which has negotiated a procurement contract with their team. Teams may subcontract, in effect, by assigning tasks to individual families, but any outside contract must be arranged with the team. Sometimes teams reimburse individual families for other services such as performing minor repairs, plaiting straw, making chopsticks or brushes, or caring for a draft animal. Always a potential bone of contention is whether individuals are devoting more than just spare time to profitable family sidelines.

Private plots. No land is privately owned in China, including residential lots, but production teams allot a small amount of their arable land to each member household for its private use. By national regulation the proportion should not exceed 5 percent, though higher proportions are found. At Huadong, the average is 4 percent; each agricultural family is allotted an average of about 1,800 square feet, or about the space needed to park eight to ten standard-sized American cars. This land may be immediately adjacent to the house, or it may be a long way off. Chances are it is one of the least fertile patches owned by the team. Families may do with their plot whatever they please. They may grow vegetables or tobacco for their own use. They may grow cash crops for market, or they may raise pigs or domestic fowl. They may not rent their land, nor may they sell it.

Even if fertility is low on private plots, however, productivity may be high (no statistics are available), because family members give tender loving care to their garden plots. Also, temptation runs high to siphon off valuable human and animal manure owned by the team to the family plot, and to devote work time expected by the team to this private pursuit.

The family of Zhang Liyi, interviewed by the New York State Educators' Study Group in 1973, was found to be farming a large private plot of 0.7 *mou* (about 0.1 acres). They were producing enough vegetables for their own use as well as a surplus for sale at the local market. All members of the family put in up to an hour of work on the plot each day after returning from their collective jobs. In addition, the Zhangs were raising a small number of pigs, which not only provided a ton of manure each per year for the vegetable plot but also brought a selling price of thirty-eight dollars each at the local market—more than twice the monthly salary of the son who worked in a coal mine. The benefits of pig raising to families are indicated by the growth of Huadong's hog population from 10,000 when the commune was founded to almost 70,000 in 1973. There are now more pigs than people in Huadong. Families know that they can increase their cash income directly by raising the output of their private plot, and that this income is untaxed.

Commerce and Markets

During the Great Leap Forward, Chinese communist

leaders were tempted by the view that all private trading is bad. At Huadong, as elsewhere, they closed the periodic "free markets" where commune members could sell home-grown produce or household manufactures. Instead, commune-managed supply and marketing cooperatives were expected to sell all items not distributed as "free supply." The results were neither surprising nor long in coming. Grave shortages of everyday goods, angry consumers, and blossoming black markets all prompted authorities to reopen the periodic markets early in the 1960s. The revived markets were supposed to be governed by "market control committees" empowered to limit hours, prices, and participants. But after a few years even critics of rural markets had come around to the pessimistic view that "closing them down by administrative order or exercising general control over them" simply would not work. The newest approach has been for the state to be more aggressive in procuring rural products so as to compete successfully with the free markets. The state's methods include (1) study, criticism, and ideological education among commune members, (2) organizing comprehensive rural trade "fairs" that feature entertaining cultural and art programs, (3) supplementing these comprehensive fairs at appropriate times with special-product fairs, and (4) urging supply and marketing cooperatives to send carts and procurement teams to villages distant from the fairgrounds (that is, to production teams far away from commune and brigade towns). One commune in northeast China boasted that, due to its success with similar policies, "the previous bourgeois practice of shouting prices and driving bargains was swept away at one stroke."[18]

At Huadong this "bourgeois practice" goes on. The Zhang family of Number 11 Team, Linong Brigade, takes vegetables from its private plot to the commune farmer's market. Most periodic markets in the vicinity convoke regularly every five days. Households like the Zhangs' with products to sell (vegetables, chickens, ducks, geese, fish,

a

b

c

PLATE 13. *a*: Clothing counter, commune department store, Tuiguang. (Robert Neiderberger) *b*: Team members market vegetables raised on their household plots. (Robert Neiderberger) *c*: Enterprising girls offer cups of hot tea for sale to passers-by. (Andrew Nathan)

snakes, dried grass for kindling, woven baskets, straw sandals and hats, and other handicraft items—dozens of products in all) like to send a member who is not a full-strength worker (usually an old person) so that they avoid losing valuable workpoints. The cash they earn amounts to only a small portion of household income. More important is the family's access to a greater variety of consumer products. Mrs. Zhang may use the money she earns selling the family's vegetables to buy a fish, a chicken, or a hat. Team and brigade representatives also bring surplus collective products to the periodic market and purchase items in short supply in their home villages.

Operating in the shadow of the law around the periodic market at Huadong is a fairly active black market. Its existence reflects shortages in the supply of goods in heaviest demand—grain, pork, fish, cotton cloth, shoes, construction materials, and others. Some black markets even proffer services such as machine repair. No official would admit to as much, but in reality local authorities do tolerate illicit black market trading as long as it does not get out of hand, that is, as long as the volume remains small and speculators do not operate regularly. Individuals who "strike out on their own" (*zou zi fa*)—by acquiring produce, ration coupons, Rolex watches, jewelry, or other products in one place and peddling them elsewhere at a profit—risk arrest and punishment. Black market transactions are conducted discreetly and are disguised as normal activity. An informant who left China in 1975 recalls price comparisons, shown in Table 3.2, in his native Zhuhai County, about fifty miles south of Hua County. Cadres responsible for finance and trade policy as high as the province level spend much of their time on the road investigating local market conditions. Their reports are forwarded regularly to central authorities in Beijing.

The socialist, or state-run, sector of trade at Huadong is the responsibility of the commune's Supply and Marketing Cooperative (SMC). This organization was built up step-by-step

TABLE 3.2

Comparison of Some List Prices and Black Market Prices, Zhuhai County, 1975

Product	List Price in $US/kilo (A)	Black Market Price in $US/kilo (B)	Ratio B/A
Fine grain rice	0.14	0.50	3.6
Unhusked rice	0.10	0.30	3.0
Grain ration coupon		0.40	
Cotton cloth ration coupon		0.18/yard	
Low quality cotton fabric	0.10/yard	0.30–0.35/yard	3–3.5
Pork	0.98	2.50–2.60	2.6
Cooking oil	0.96	2.80	2.9
Granulated sugar (sha tang)	0.45	0.56	1.2
Cooking sugar (pian tang)	0.30	0.45–0.50	1.5

through mergers of village coops formed after land reform. About 1956, all the coops in Hua County merged into a single county-wide SMC under the supervision of the County Commerce Department. Two years later when the communes were created, employees of the Hua County SMC who worked in Beixia and Tuiguang simply were transferred to the Huadong SMC. The chairman of Huadong's Revolutionary Committee, Xu Yunchen, once worked for the supply and marketing coop at Huaxian. The commune SMC is still subordinate to the County Commerce Department, through which it does most of its ordering, but in its local activity the staff is responsible to the Huadong Revolutionary Committee. The Huadong SMC serves two important functions: it purchases what the commune produces through a network of procurement stations and points, and it supplies what commune members need through a network of shops.

On the purchasing side, the SMC actively stimulates output of products in demand. Staff members investigate the relative merits of available insecticides and farm equipment, in consultation with growers and experimenters, and lay in timely supplies. They make advance purchasing agreements with teams and brigades. They help brigades start up small sidelines, for example by supplying saplings for a new orchard or grinding machines to process wild medicinal herbs that brigade members gather. Also, they act as procurement agents for the County Commerce Department. Their rice, pork, peanut, vegetable, fruit, and other purchases may end up in retail shops in Chinese cities, or they may be exported. SMC personnel often set up temporary "procurement points" in brigades and mobile points in distant teams for the convenience of these out-of-the-way producers.

On the supply side, the SMC manages several shops in the commune town. A large one-room general store offers textiles, clothes, housewares, sporting goods, books, and other items. Among the books are a selection of children's stories and thick "barefoot doctor" texts. A pharmacy offers both traditional Chinese medicines and Western medicines in separate departments. Other specialty shops offer farm implements, cameras and photo supplies, bicycles, and radios. There are simple restaurants and an "ice room" for snacks. Small peddlers hawk additional wares on the street, but they are rather few in comparison with Hongkong, especially considering the throngs of shoppers who regularly crowd the Tuiguang town streets.

The SMC runs smaller branch stores in many brigade towns. These more accessible shops handle most daily necessities, but shoppers still prefer the commune town for variety. A favorite outing on holidays is a bus ride to Huaxian, the county seat, or even to the big city Guangzhou, where shopping is best of all. Huadong young people sometimes make the round trip to Guangzhou by bicycle.

SMC personnel make efforts to learn what products Huadong residents would like to have on the shelves in greater quantity or variety. And they make timely preparations to stock in special holiday items for the New Year and other festive occasions.

Work Compensation: Egalitarianism versus Incentives

A central target of socialist critiques of capitalist society is the liberal assumption that individuals ought to be free to gain as much as possible for themselves on the strength of their own brains, hard effort, and personal sacrifice. Socialists argue that such a system left unchecked leads to permanent inequalities in the form of social classes. People born to higher classes then cling to their privileges, and people born to lower classes find that they have correspondingly fewer opportunities to realize their potential. That is, lower class people come to be exploited by higher class people and by "liberal democratic" government. Socialists believe that too much inequality is bad, because the rich always will take advantage of the poor.

CCP doctrine views some inequality as necessary during the long historical transition to communism. The question is how much. Some inequality in income increases farm labor productivity by rewarding those who work harder and strengthens the collective ownership system by reducing the attractiveness of alternative private pursuits or migration to the city. Too much inequality in income, however, can weaken the collective ownership system by encouraging people to work mainly for themselves. It favors households with more able-bodied workers over those with fewer workers and more children, old people, and disabled or chronically ill persons. It also fosters undesirable "bourgeois" thinking by making possible sharply contrasting living standards. The search for the proper amount of income inequality has produced repeated experimentation and lively debate at Huadong.

The collective income each household receives depends on (1) the team's total income at distribution time, (2) the portion of that total remaining after deductions are made for the team's taxes, required grain sales to the state, seed for the next crop, animal feed, grain storage, investment fund deposit, and welfare fund contribution, and (3) the criteria for dividing this remaining portion (which at Huadong averages about 50 percent) among individual team members. The "shareout" after grain harvests is paid partly in kind and partly in cash. Shares of team income from vegetables or other collective sideline production may be paid in cash monthly. Households earn additional cash from their own sidelines such as raising pigs or making sandals. Such items are sold to a commune procurement station (pigs) or at the commune periodic market (sandals).

Back in 1958, the most common compensation policy adopted by the early communes combined "free supply" with a wage system like the eight-grade system used in factories. About 60 percent of the "shareout" would be given to individuals "according to need." This was the "free supply" part. The other 40 percent would be given "according to work" as wages to commune workers who were "graded" according to their skill level. That is, a grade six peasant laborer would receive more wages for a day's work than one at grade five, irrespective of the task. The problem was that while industrial workers typically perform a few repetitive tasks, peasants typically perform many varying ones (hauling rocks, transplanting seedlings, weeding, spraying insecticides, tending cattle, and so on).

By the early 1960s, many important changes had occurred to overcome practical problems with the free supply/wage system. Newly important "production teams" drastically reduced their free supply proportion to 30 percent or less and devised several systems to reward individual team members who worked harder than their fellows. Many people even wanted to withdraw from collectives, but this "trend of going it alone" was eventually contained. Practices followed by teams differed, but commonly team leaders would rate each member primarily by skill in terms of workpoints per day for normal tasks. An able-bodied man might be rated at ten workpoints a day, a woman at eight, a notorious slacker at seven and a half, and someone who had been caught stealing from the team granary at just seven. The most difficult tasks might be rated separately, making it possible for volunteers to earn fourteen workpoints a day hauling rocks. Some tasks might be paid by time (tending cattle) and others paid by the amount of work completed (weeding). Finally, the brigade or commune would sometimes grant compensatory workpoints to a team whose members were temporarily transferred to outside tasks—helping with road or canal repair, attending tractor driving and repair school, serving as a schoolteacher or barefoot doctor, participating in commune-level meetings, and so on. Bewildering complexity characterized these policies, and many teams had real trouble keeping account of their workpoints, time rates, overtime rates, piece rates, cash reward payments, and compensatory arrangements.

About 1965 some Guangdong Province communes began experimenting with the "Dazhai workpoint system," which brought three innovations. First, separate tasks were no longer singled out for separate compensation. Second, individuals would be rated by comprehensive criteria (political thought, attitude toward labor, technical skill, and productivity) and paid accordingly for a day's work at any task. Third, these ratings would be reviewed once a month by the team as a whole. Members would discuss each person's self-evaluation, making whatever revisions they deemed appropriate. Late in the Cultural Revolution (1966-1969), during which those taking the "capitalist road" were vigorously criticized and "material incentives" were brought under heavy fire, the Dazhai workpoint system was popularized and higher free supply proportions were revived.

By 1970 the pendulum had again swung away from these more egalitarian experiments, as it had in the early 1960s. Teams reduced their per capita distributions and reinstituted both task rates and time rates. Many teams that had adopted the Dazhai workpoint system abandoned it. The Dazhai system remained the ideal at Huadong as elsewhere in China, but its implementation was eventually understood to be a sensitive process that must respect team conditions and win the approval of team members.

Experimentation continues because each work compensation policy has both strengths and weaknesses. Per capita allocations operate like welfare, benefitting families with low labor power. One important benefit is allowing such families to overdraw and go into debt to their team in years when their income is low. The Dazhai workpoint system offers advantages for progressive teams with relative equality among member households, good cooperative spirit, and strong leadership. In less progressive teams, however, the vagueness of the Dazhai criteria causes tedious disputes in the early rating discussions and brings personal and kinship animosities to the surface. Moreover, once ratings have been settled, these teams seek to avoid further conflict by reaffirming the initial ratings month after month. Participation in the monthly review meetings declines, especially among poor and lower-middle peasants who feel that their ratings are secure. As people are paid on the basis of class labels and initial ratings, rather than for their previous month's performance as judged by Dazhai standards, the system loses its intended incentive effects. Finally, young activists tend to be upgraded under the Dazhai system, which arouses resentments among older peasants and the "five black elements." The system of cadre-assigned workpoint ratings, coupled with piece-rate systems, strongly benefits households with higher labor power.

The Jiang Family of Linong Brigade: A Portrait

Mr. and Mrs. Jiang, their son, his wife and seven children live in a ninety-year-old house that has been in the family for five generations. The brick dwelling, part of a larger complex of buildings housing several families, has been enlarged to accommodate the eleven members of the Jiang family. The buildings and accompanying trees present a low profile among the expanse of rice paddies in which they are located.

a

c

PLATE 14. *a*: Mr. and Mrs. Jiang are at back right. To their right are their daughter-in-law and son. The other four girls and two boys are their grandchildren. One married daughter lives with her family in another brigade. Their oldest grandson has left to join the army. (Robert Neiderberger) *b*: In the Jiangs' kitchen, facing the wall with the stove. (Robert Neiderberger) *c*: Their large stove and fuel bin. (Robert Neiderberger) *d*: Mr. and Mrs. Jiang with the elaborate luncheon their son has prepared for visiting members of the New York State Educators' Study Group. Ordinarily they would eat a much plainer midday meal. (Robert Neiderberger)

b

d

102

a

c

PLATE 15. *a*: A granddaughter draws water from the well in the courtyard. (Robert Neiderberger) *b*: The canopied bed. (Robert Neiderberger)
c: Their living room, looking toward the wall with the table. The loft

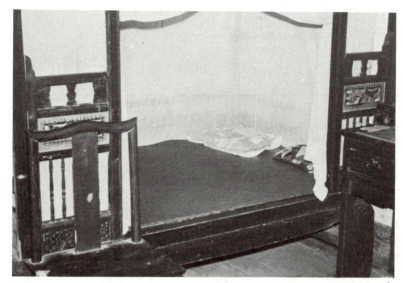

b

d

is visible at the top. (Robert Neiderberger) *d*: The building complex
that includes their house. The people are some of the Jiangs' neighbors.
(Robert Neiderberger)

FIGURE 3.1

Floor Plan of Jiang Family Home, Huadong Commune

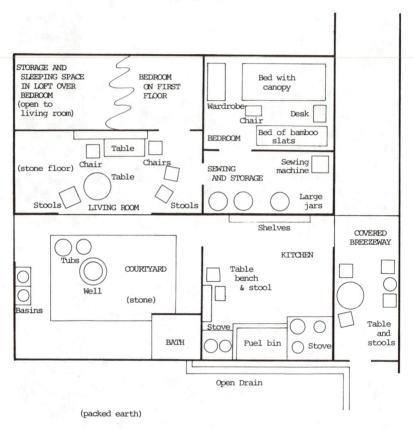

(packed earth)

Source: Adapted from Teaching about the People's Republic of China (Albany, N.Y.: New York State Education Department, 1975), p. 61. All of the information about the Jiang family in this section was collected by L. Heidi Hursh, Robert Neiderberger, and Elaine Zanicchi of the New York State Educators' Study Group.

The kitchen is entered from the outside through a roofed passageway (see Figure 3.1). It is a large, rather dark room. One end of the kitchen doubles as an entrance to the rest of the living quarters. Cooking utensils are arranged along the walls. A bin between the stoves contains straw and other fuel. The several small wooden benches and tables in the kitchen were made by Mr. Jiang.

The other rooms are reached by going through a small

courtyard containing the well, a raised circular opening in the courtyard's stone floor. The plentiful water supply a few feet down is reached with a wooden bucket suspended from a pole. Other buckets, tubs, and basins are scattered about the courtyard. A walled-in bathing facility is located in one corner.

The large living room, although without windows, is adequately lighted by daylight streaming through the open doorway. As in the other rooms, there is no ceiling save the open rafters and roof beams. The floor is made of square stones and the walls of painted plaster. In addition to the furniture—two small tables, four chairs, and several low stools—the following items are seen about the room:

> Mirror
> Collection of family photos in frames
>   made by Mr. Jiang
> Portrait of Mao Zedong
> Poster of Beijing Opera
> Calendar
> Large pendulum clock
> Plaster bust of Mao
> Gold fish
> 2 large vacuum bottles
>   containing boiled water
>   for drinking
> 2 framed citations from the PLA
>   awarded to the son
> Farm tools
> 3 bicycles
> 3 raincoats
> Radio (mounted in wall)
> Electric light
> Hooks for hanging kerosene lamps
> 3 canteens
> Canvas bags
> Plants

The overall appearance is orderly. Beyond the living room is a bedroom, over which is a storage loft open to the living room under the roof rafters. This upper area doubles as a sleeping area for Mr. and Mrs. Jiang.

To one side of the living room is a small room with a sewing machine and various containers for storing food. Large pots contain grain husks, food for ducks and chickens, squash, various kinds of roots, and sauces essential to the cooking style of the area. One poster of Beijing and another of the ''Red Lantern'' revolutionary ballet adorn the walls.

Mr. Jiang is a sixty-five-year-old retired carpenter. His wife, who is sixty, no longer works in the fields. The Jiangs' forty-year-old son works at a grain-husking mill on another commune. He stays at the factory for the work week and returns home on his rest day. Their daughter-in-law, also forty, works in the fields of Linong Brigade. The Jiangs have a married daughter living with her husband in another brigade of Huadong. The Jiangs have six grandchildren living in the house, not including the oldest grandson, nineteen, who recently left to join the army. The oldest girl is a middle school graduate who works in the fields. Another girl is in her second year of junior middle school. There are two girls in primary school, and two boys who are not yet school age.

In a conversation with members of the New York State Educators' Study Group, Mr. Jiang offered these observations on his lifestyle:

> I have been a carpenter for a long time. I was a carpenter before Liberation, but I recall that life was bitter in those years. I did not have steady work, and even when I did work my income was small. Often I worked as a laborer in the fields. During those years I didn't make enough to support a wife and two children. To make things worse, my anxiety and misery led me to a bad habit. On paydays I would buy opium and smoke it. Life had no guarantees except worry. For instance, I worried that someone in our family might get sick. There was no place to turn to for help and medical costs were high.
>
> However, all this has changed since Liberation. In 1952 I found work in Guangzhou and visited home on my rest days. I broke the habit of smoking opium. When the commune was

established, medicine and medical care were provided. Now I am retired on 70 percent of my former salary and I live here with my family on the commune. This house we live in has been in our family for generations. Once a month I go back to Guangzhou to attend a study group.

My wife and I live upstairs over our son's family. My wife and my daughter-in-law share many of the household chores. In some activities my wife takes control. Since she is retired and no longer works in the fields, she assumes responsibility for many household chores. When my daughter-in-law gets home from the fields, and her daughters get home from school, they all pitch in with the housework. My wife takes care of the family's finances but she doesn't refuse to give money to one who asks. Although it is rarely necessary, my wife is also responsible for disciplining the children since our son is away most of the time and our daughter-in-law works.

My daily routine begins about 5:00 or 5:30 in the morning when I get up and go to the teahouse to meet with my friends and drink. By 7:00 I am back here at the house and involved with taking care of the youngest children. I spend some time each day building tables, chairs, or doors. Sometimes I repair furniture for our family or for the neighbors. I made most of the furniture we own. My wife fixes lunch around noon. After lunch I rest until about 2:30. I continue with my carpentry in the afternoon or else talk with my neighbors. We eat dinner at 6:00. After dinner I read the newspaper or listen to the radio and then go to bed around 8:00.

Because this house was ours before the Liberation we do not pay rent. As members of Huadong Commune we receive a private plot of land totaling 0.6 *mou* (0.1 acre). The amount of land given to a family varies with its size. Grain, cereal, and firewood are provided by the Linong Production Brigade. We spend the most money per year—about 20 yuan [$10] each—on clothing. Other important expenditures include meat and sauces. Our total expenditure per year, not including grain, is 600 yuan [$300]. We save money for different things we want to buy. We've managed to buy three bicycles, a sewing machine, and a radio.

It is well past noon and you must be hungry. Since today is my son's day off from work, he has prepared lunch for us all. Shall we have something to eat?

Family Income and Standard of Living

By 1973 the average family income at Huadong had risen above $350, a level six times higher than the early 1950s figure, and five times higher than it was when the commune was founded. This represents a real increase in purchasing power, since retail prices have been relatively stable since 1953. The average income of Huadong families is slightly above the national average. Individual wealth varies somewhat by team and by family. Teams whose geographical location brings them such advantages as better land or better irrigation, or who enjoy better leadership, may earn up to three or four times as much per family as poorer teams. Also, families with more labor power, more education, and more diligence may earn considerably more than their less fortunate, less skilled, or less energetic neighbors in the same team.

Still, after all is considered, differences between the richest and poorest families in Huadong, or even in all of China, are not nearly so great as the gap between rich and poor in the United States, Western Europe, or Japan. This egalitarian factor is significant because it means that "keeping up with the Chens" in Huadong is easier than keeping up with the Joneses in Austin. Huadong families save their cash income for a watch, camera, transistor radio, sewing machine, bicycle, occasional new clothes, basic home improvements or house building, a little extra food, small entertainments, infrequent long-distance travel by train, boat or bus, medical plan contribution, and perhaps rent of 2 to 4 percent of monthly income or school fees of three or four dollars per year per child. Middle-class consumerism of the Western or Japanese sort, when contrasted with consumption levels in any poorer agricultural society in the world, China being simply one case, resembles an excited fantasy by a mad science fiction writer. Most Western and Japanese families can purchase uncountably more things than Chinese families can purchase (see Table 3.3), but most of this consumption is

TABLE 3.3

Relative Consumer Purchasing Power in China and the United States, 1974

Commodity	Working Time Required for Purchase		Ratio, China/U.S. (of unrounded figures)
	In China	In the U.S.	
	No. hours: min.	No. hours: min.	
1 pound rice	0:30	0:04	7/1
1 pound chicken	3:51	0:12	26/1
1 pound white sugar	2:16	0:03	46/1
	No. weeks/days	No. hours: min.	
1 square meter cotton print	0/1	0:30	18/1
Good quality blue cotton work shirt	0/2	2:30	6/1
Light wool sweater	1/3	5:00	15/1
Bicycle	2/4	6:00	23/1
Small transistor radio	0/4	0:30	53/1
Domestic wristwatch	1/6	1:30	60/1

Source: Adapted from Alexander Eckstein, China's Economic Revolution (New York: Cambridge University Press, 1977), p. 306. Eckstein assumes for his comparisons that the average Chinese wage is $30/month and the average U.S. wage $591/month.

well beyond survival, or even status, needs by world standards.

While the income of Huadong families is just a fraction of that of Western or Japanese families, they also need to spend only a fraction as much for other necessities, such as housing. Although Huadong families would like to buy more food, more varieties of food, more cotton cloth, more construction materials, and more consumer durables, their relative poverty is not so great as income statistics alone might suggest. Eighty percent of Huadong families have personal savings on deposit with the credit cooperative, and the amount of their savings has grown impressively. In 1953 the commune area attracted only $21,000 of personal bank deposits, but by 1973 the sum had risen to $705,000, an unknown portion of which may be remittances from relatives abroad. At the end of 1976 the reported figure stood at $900,000. As soon as China has more consumer goods to offer on rural markets, the people of Huadong undoubtedly will divert some of their rising income and higher savings to consumer spending. There are no formal restrictions on what individuals may do with their money, and there is no inheritance tax on property willed to relatives. The People's Bank and credit cooperatives do not grant consumer loans, however, so all such purchases must be saved for in advance.

In 1973 one delegation member recorded the following observations from a visit with the Zhang family of Number 11 Team, Linong Brigade.[19] Much larger than the average Huadong household of five, the Zhang family has thirteen members living together in three houses. Seven are income earners: the Zhangs' "labor power" in the production team is four, two are "workers" in other commune enterprises, and one attends to family sideline production.

Mr. Zhang Liyi	Team farmworker (labor power)
Mrs. Zhang (illiterate)	Manages family sidelines and family finances including salaries of working members

a

b

PLATE 16. *a*: Office of the commune credit cooperative. (Andrew Nathan) *b*: Teller. (Andrew Nathan)

Son No. 1	Worker in coal mine (worker)
Daughter-in-law	Team farmworker (labor power)
Daughter No. 1	Sales girl in commune general store (worker)
Daughter No. 2	Team farmworker (labor power)
Daughter No. 3	Team farmworker (labor power)
Son No. 2	Senior middle school student
Daughter No. 4	Senior middle school student
Son No. 3	Primary school student
Daughter No. 5	Primary school student
Grandson No. 1	Preschooler
Grandson No. 2	Preschooler

The Zhangs built their house in 1962 for $150. They were able to use some materials from their old clay house. The walls are high and made of brick, and both the roof and floor are tiled. They did all the construction work themselves. Over the years they have made several improvements as savings permitted and as construction materials were available. The house is waterproof and relatively comfortable. It now has five sections, each with a sitting room, and two other small houses have been added next door. Outside are six chicken coops, along with a cat, dog, and chicks. Two bicycles are parked in the front room. One kitchen serves for all. Water is drawn from a well in the courtyard. In one corner stands a sewing machine powered by a foot pedal. Walls are adorned with theater posters advertising *The Red Lantern* and *The White-Haired Girl.* Many family photos are displayed, most of them portraits. Several are group photos, apparently of school classes. A picture shows Chairman Mao visiting the Guangzhou Paper Factory, and a quotation from Chairman Mao is pasted on a mirror. The furniture is very plain; benches are positioned about a low, round table. The buildings are considered the Zhangs' private property and would remain with the family even if some members were to die or move away. The Zhangs are permitted to rent or sell, but this is rarely done.

Mr. Zhang is dressed in black shorts and a brown jacket. Mrs. Zhang is dressed in a long-sleeved black shirt and black trousers. One son wears blue shorts and an undershirt. All are barefoot, except for one daughter, who is wearing green trousers, a blue cotton shirt, and sandals.

Mrs. Zhang says that last year (1972) the four team workers together earned $490, most of it paid in kind with 3,100 kilograms of rice. The coal miner earned $222, and the salesgirl brought in $195. Another $150 came from the sale of four pigs to the commune purchasing station. A few more dollars were garnered from sales of vegetables on the free market. The total was about $1,100, roughly 15 percent of which (and about 25 percent of the cash part) was accounted for by the sale of pigs and vegetables. The Zhangs' private plot of 0.1 acre is located several hundred yards from the house. Mrs. Zhang works on it up to an hour a day. In addition to the small surplus of produce for market, the plot provides all vegetables consumed by the family and fodder for the pigs.

Mrs. Zhang, describing the family's expenditures, says that they live a quiet villager's life. They raise their own chickens, eggs, vegetables, and tobacco. The rice received from the team is more than they eat, and about 250 kilograms per year is set aside "against time of war or natural calamity." All they really need buy at the village store is fish at twenty cents per kilogram and pork at forty cents. The family's coal miner is allotted a grain ration of forty-five kilograms per month, and its sales girl thirty. This they would buy from the team at ten cents per kilogram.

Both economic growth rates and equity of income distribution in China are far ahead of their performance levels a generation ago. Interpretations of China's record of progress vary considerably, but few observers doubt that the progress so far is real. The most important question now is whether it can be sustained.

Suggested Reading

Grain Farming

National Academy of Sciences, *Plant Studies in the People's Republic of China* (Washington, D.C., 1975).

Dwight H. Perkins, *Agricultural Development in China, 1368-1968* (Chicago: Aldine, 1969).

Benedict Stavis, *Making Green Revolution: The Politics of Agricultural Development in China* (Ithaca, N.Y.: Center for International Studies, Cornell University, 1974).

Enterprises, Sidelines, and Private Plots

Dwight Perkins, ed., *Rural Small-Scale Industry in the People's Republic of China* (Berkeley and Los Angeles: University of California Press, 1977).

Jon Sigurdson, *Rural Industrialization in China* (Cambridge, Mass.: Harvard University Press, 1977).

Commerce and Markets

Gordon Bennett, *China's Finance and Trade: A Policy Reader* (White Plains, N.Y.: M.E. Sharpe, 1978).

Audrey Donnithorne, *China's Economic System* (New York: Praeger, 1967).

Dwight H. Perkins, *Market Control and Planning in Communist China* (Cambridge, Mass.: Harvard University Press, 1966).

G. William Skinner, "Marketing and Social Structure in Rural China," pts. 1-3, *Journal of Asian Studies* 24, nos. 1-3 (November 1964, February 1965, May 1965).

Work Compensation: Egalitarianism versus Incentives

Charles Hoffmann, *Work Incentive Practices and Policies in the People's Republic of China, 1953-1965* (Albany: State University of New York Press, 1967).

Carl Riskin, "Maoism and Motivation: Work Incentives in China," *Bulletin of Concerned Asian Scholars* 5, no. 1 (July 1973): 10-24; reprinted in Victor Nee and James Peck, eds., *China's Uninterrupted Revolution: From 1840 to the Present* (New York: Pantheon, 1975), pp. 415-461.

Family Income and Standard of Living

Wilfred Burchett with Rewi Alley, *China: The Quality of Life* (Baltimore, Md.: Penguin Books, 1976).

4
Society

It has not been possible for Chinese society to reject the strong revolutionary currents of the twentieth century. At the same time, even the forces of revolution have not been able to subdue a social system many centuries in the making. Some would say that the resulting mixture of the old and the new is a compromised new; others would say it is a rejuvenated old.

Population began to grow once again after peace was restored in the 1950s, but more recently the rate of growth has responded to official efforts to control it. Every aspect of population policy is terribly important in China, which has roughly four times as many people as the United States. China's total national income (GNP) is only about one-tenth that of the United States, making per capita GNP in China only about one-fortieth as large. Another major problem area has been adequate public health; families have little to spend on medical care, and the government has little to invest in training and equipping doctors. Yet, making the best of what they do have, the authorities have devised several very innovative health care programs. The women's movement in China is very active in spite of the absence of liaison with similar movements in other countries; as Huadong Commune data illustrate well, barriers to equality for women are stronger in the countryside than in the city. China's education system has progressed to a point where universal literacy is claimed for everyone under age forty-five. Many lively debates continue, however, over admissions criteria, curricula, organization of research, and other questions. A social sphere that shows little evidence of change is friendship and recreation, where people find havens from the pressures of work and revolutionary politics.

Population

The Huadong area's population grew from 36,000 in 1949 to 61,000 in 1973, an average annual increase rate of 2.2 percent. Commune officials told visitors in the early 1970s that their immediate goal was to reduce the growth rate to 1.9 percent. Assuming that they had succeeded at this by 1973 and could further reduce the rate to 1.3 percent by 1980 and 1.0 percent by 1990, the original 1949 population would double to 72,000 by 1983 (a thirty-four-year interval) and double again to 144,000 by 2051 (a sixty-eight-year interval). The work force in 1973 was 28,000, 85 percent full-time and 15 percent part-time.

Controlling the rate of increase was not considered a problem in the early years of the commune system, incredible as this might sound for a country with four times the population of the United States. The gloomy predictions of Thomas Malthus, to the effect that the earth's people increase faster than the earth's food supply and that famine is inevitable unless disease and war keep the world's population in check, were ridiculed in Chinese statements of the time. Such dire consequences, maintained the Party leadership, were the result of "capitalist exploitation." Under "socialism," food production could increase rapidly. This ideological position never has been repudiated outright. Nonetheless, China has moved gradually toward effective population control policies.

One policy is to encourage late marriage, in the hope that

the delay will mean fewer children. The ideal marriage age for women now is twenty-three to twenty-five, for men twenty-five to twenty-eight. This standard is not rigidly enforced. Some young people at Huadong do conform to the ideal, but many still marry in their early twenties. Another policy is active distribution of birth control literature and aids. Newly married couples (but only married couples) are given a booklet explaining the different techniques. In practice, most of the burden still falls on the woman. In the early 1970s, visitors were told that 80 percent of Huadong's women of childbearing age (it was not clear, but likely, that just married women were meant) practiced some method of birth control. About half of them used pills and about half used intra-uterine devices. Some men used condoms. Sterilization is extremely rare. Abortion is available on demand but is not encouraged, and if the woman is unmarried, she must undergo a program of "education."

Strong mores and lack of privacy discourage premarital sex in China, and in fact the incidence of illegitimate births is low. The Marriage Law stipulates that "children born out of wedlock shall enjoy the same rights as children born in lawful wedlock," suggesting that illegitimacy was a source of stigma in the past and probably still is today. In Huadong, however, this is a minor social problem. Young people usually socialize in groups, and going off alone with a girlfriend or boyfriend is rare and considered a bit "wild."

Parents or other older relatives often encourage young married couples to have more children than the government advocates and encourage the addition of boys to the family. They argue that the family's welfare will increase with more male "labor power" to contribute to the team. They also argue that the welfare of elderly parents remains primarily the responsibility of their sons. Cadres answer these concerns with several arguments. First, the commune's control over epidemics and natural disasters means that more "full labor power" sons will survive than in the old days. Second, fewer children mean fewer mouths to feed. Third, old age security now is partly the responsibility of the collective. In 1973, 193 orphans and old people without families received the "five guarantees" from their team (food, clothes, medical care, education, and funeral). The official position is slowly prevailing, and family size is decreasing, but in the mid-1970s many rural Huadong families still had three or more children. The average family size in 1973 was five, and the average number of workers in each family was 2.3, a relatively high proportion.

Food consumption in Huadong, according to a careful estimate by Claude Aubert, probably averaged 2,600 calories per day in 1973. Aubert's estimate rests on the assumptions that the average monthly grain ration to each individual was 23.5 kilograms, that after milling losses this left 600 grams per day for consumption (2100 calories), and that the cereal portion of the average diet was 82 percent.[20] The average daily food intake has been increasing slowly, but in future years food supply will be a serious problem unless more efficient fertilizer application and agricultural mechanization result in dramatic increases in food production per acre. Huadong officials, however, are optimistic. They point out that Guangdong Province as a whole became self-sufficient in grain in 1953, and that the area later incorporated into Huadong People's Commune began to sell a surplus to the government in 1957. In 1973 Huadong delivered a surplus of 35 percent of its total grain harvest to the state, either as agricultural tax (5 percent) or as sales (30 percent).

In 1972, the only year for which we have complete statistics, Huadong recorded 1,492 births and 357 deaths. This was a "natural increase" of 1,135. The total increase, however, was 1,669, or 534 more than the natural increase. This means that 534 more people moved into the commune in 1972 than moved out. Some of the immigrants were "down-to the villages youth" (see below).

Much immigration and emigration is explained by Huadong's proximity to Guangzhou, a metropolis of almost 3 million people and China's principal southern city. Not only because of its long and colorful history and its overseas contacts, but also because of its unique role in China's foreign trade and its intricate relations with the nearby British colony of Hongkong, Guangzhou is considered *fuza,* "complicated." With its promise of higher wages, better living conditions, more interesting job opportunities, and hopes of upward mobility, Guangzhou is a glittering lure to the rural youth of Huadong. Over the years a whole host of government policies designed to stem the flow of ambitious young people from farm to factory has met with only uneven success. When migration into the city was outlawed, many young people showed a willingness to break the law. Denying them regular employment was not the answer: they could find temporary jobs or other irregular employment. Refusing illegal city dwellers food and cotton ration coupons did not work: they could find a shopkeeper who would sell these necessities without the coupons. Nor was it possible to bar them from housing: they could move in with friends or relatives. At least two efforts to round them up forcibly and return them to their home villages were ineffective, because they simply returned to Guangzhou as soon as official concern had shifted to some new problem.

Migration to rural areas began in earnest after the Cultural Revolution (1966-1969). As part of a broad, nationwide effort to reduce the gap between city and countryside, a serious campaign was launched to settle educated city youth (mostly middle school graduates) in rural areas. Since 1968 more than 12 million educated youth have been resettled. The idea started before the Cultural Revolution as a vehicle for "rusticating" city boys and girls—that is, reforming their outlook by removing them from the comforts of city life and sending them to the school of hard knocks in the poorer countryside where 80 percent of China's people live and struggle to survive. It was also a way of reducing demands for higher education and employment in comfortable white collar jobs. Over the years the idea has matured. Now, in addition to the "rustication" of participating youth, a secondary objective is to improve the lot of the host teams and brigades through incorporation of new intellectual talent and youthful aspiration.

By 1971 Huadong had received 273 "down-to-the-villages youth," and three years later the total was 517. Most came from Guangzhou. Some teams hosted several, some teams none. New arrivals would typically live with a peasant family until they could build their own houses. To ease the host team's burden, the government gave each settler 430 yuan (a little over $200) to contribute to construction costs. Of the 1974 total of 517 educated city youth, 387 have remained in the commune and 130 have left. Of the ones who stayed, 13 very quickly became production team leaders, a few more advanced to brigade cadre, 10 became scientific workers, 1 an accountant, 1 a cashier, 1 a broadcast announcer, 2 became barefoot doctors, 8 became teachers, and 3 became technicians at a commune mill. In time, we expect that many of the others will also rise to positions of responsibility, mainly because of their higher literacy and ability with figures. Nineteen have settled down and established families in the commune. Of the 130 who left Huadong, 3 joined the army, 3 were admitted to a university, 16 were accepted at a technical school, 81 were recruited to work in state-owned enterprises or in government offices, and 27 left due to marriage or other reasons. Relationships between peasants and educated city youth have varied widely. Sometimes they get along well. Then, the young people learn to appreciate their host's life situation and strive to be helpful, and peasants respond to their efforts warmly. In other cases, the city youth look down upon the peasants as slow and dull, and the peasants look down upon the city youth as spoiled and arrogant. Occasionally time helps to bridge the "urban-rural gap" but not always.

While it is true that most of Huadong's population (94 percent) are village farmers tilling the soil as part of a production team, a variety of jobs and social roles characterizes this complex community. In addition to plain agricultural laborers, each team has cadres, a political instructor, a women's work leader, representatives to the brigade assembly, maybe a few political activists, veteran skilled farmers, young inexperienced farmers, a tractor driver/repairman, a health worker, demobilized soldiers, "down-to-the-villages youth," young people away at technical school or university, young people in the army, children, old people assigned child care and domestic chores, women working at collective sidelines, militia members, performing arts troupe members, players on sports teams, individuals who contribute little to the team and pursue private undertakings instead, "elements under current supervision," and the sick and disabled. The list grows longer at the brigade and commune levels. Town dwellers living at the commune center, Tuiguang, belong to no production team at all. And the northern hills are populated mainly by the Hakka minority, the so-called "guest people" who migrated in from northern China many centuries earlier but still retain their own speech and customs.

Public Health and Medical Care

Chinese ingenuity is strikingly evident in the area of public health and medical care. Over the last two decades, authorities have managed to introduce no less than five new major health policies, and people responsible for health care in China are justifiably proud of their achievements. First, they have made epidemic control and disease prevention a priority. Brigade health stations distribute traditional herbal preparations designed to ward off heat stroke in summer, enteritis and dysentery in autumn, and influenza in winter. In spring, they give children medicine to guard against measles. In their immunization program, county health departments may supply to those who need them vaccines or preventive medicines against such diseases as smallpox, diphtheria, whooping cough, epidemic meningitis, encephalitis, undulant fever, tetanus, measles, typhoid fever, malaria, and polio. These are distributed free of charge by commune clinics to brigade health stations. In 1970, Huadong doctors gave every commune member a general checkup, including a tuberculosis examination. From time to time, authorities organize mass campaigns to propagate public health and sanitation measures, to kill flies, and to make "five improvements" (in latrines, pigsties, wells, stoves, and the general environment). Especially emphasized are making excreta harmless to health, ensuring the purity of drinking water, and keeping kitchens hygienic. As a result, infectious diseases are very rare. What is more, opium addiction and venereal disease have been wiped out by all reports.

Second, the Chinese have revived their traditional medicine. Instead of regarding all ancient techniques as superstitious, and all traditional doctors (more than 750,000 existed in the 1950s) as quacks, the government has promoted experimental research to determine which of the old ways might still have a legitimate place in modern healing. As a result, acupuncture, some herbal medicines, and several other traditional practices are once again officially encouraged and widely used. Traditional medicine is often cheaper, is available to more people, and is preferred. Of the sixteen doctors at the Huadong Commune Hospital, four practice traditional medicine alone, while the other twelve practice both traditional and Western-style medicine.

Third, the Chinese have shifted the focus of medical care to the countryside. Huadong's hospital was built in 1958 as one of the commune's first projects. It is a three-story poured concrete building with an operating room, x-ray room, physiotherapy room with a heat lamp, maternity ward, consulting room, laboratory, and small shop for manufacturing

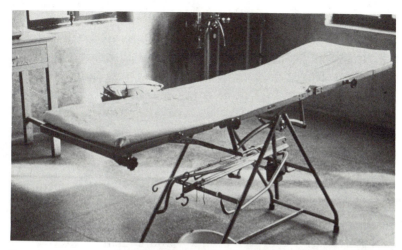

a

b

PLATE 17. *a*: The operating table in the commune hospital at Tuiguang. (Robert Neiderberger) *b*: The hospital's 13 mA x-ray machine, manufactured in Guangzhou. (Robert Neiderberger)

medicines. The hospital had forty-six beds in 1973 and had an addition under construction. The rooms are small and not air-conditioned, but they are technically adequate. The staff of sixty-five in 1973 included thirteen nurses, and more were being recruited and trained. After Chairman Mao's June 1965 criticism of the Ministry of Health as the "Ministry of Health for Urban Overlords" and his accompanying instruction ("In medical and health work put the stress on rural areas"), five doctors were transferred from Guangzhou to Huadong. The first surgeon arrived in 1967, and in 1970 the operating theater was improved. In 1970, 130 major operations were performed, including pancreas and stomach operations, caesarian sections, hysterectomies, and abortions. More complicated kidney and lung operations are referred to Guangzhou. Huadong has no blood bank yet; instead, a current registry of volunteer donors is kept. During regular hours, six or seven doctors are on duty, and two are on duty round the clock. Hospital staff see about five hundred outpatients a day, half of them children. The most common ailments at Huadong are children's stomach troubles and colic fever due to the weather.

Another of the hospital's activities is helping brigades manage their own "health stations." Commune doctors make regular rounds among the brigades. More important, however, the hospital trains successive classes of "barefoot doctors." These paramedics start with just a few months of training but gradually expand it to two years or more. They learn to perform simple medical techniques themselves, and they are taught to recognize more serious maladies that should be referred to the commune hospital. Brigade health stations are connected to the hospital by telephone, and six trucks are designated for emergency service as ambulances. Being chosen for barefoot doctor training is considered quite an honor among brigade members, and considerable prestige is earned by the young people who do the job well. A few of them are eventually able to go on to medical school. Barefoot doctors work at least half time in the fields. By 1973 each brigade had three or four barefoot doctors, but the number is growing as each new class is graduated. Each brigade also has three or four midwives, and most births take place at home. Production teams like to have one of their members designated as a "health worker" to provide simple ministrations in spare time. Brigade health stations support the efforts of these volunteers.

Fourth, the Chinese have kept the cost of medical care low. Prices of many medicines have actually fallen over the years. In August 1969, a nationwide round of pharmaceutical price cuts brought the average cost of medicine for Huadong residents down to about 20 percent of what it had been in 1950. Now, for example, one shot of penicillin at Huadong costs nine cents. Prices of medical instruments and equipment, reagents, vaccines, and blood plasma have also been reduced. While we have no specific figures for Huadong, elsewhere in China a birth delivery costs about two dollars and fifty cents, an appendectomy or hernia repair four dollars, and chest or brain surgery fifteen dollars.

Finally, the Chinese have popularized a cooperative medical insurance plan for rural families in the 1970s. The plan is managed by brigades. Each year every person pays a one dollar premium, and their team contributed a matching amount. Brigades set their own rules, but on the average medicines are free to participating members up to a limit of five to fifteen dollars. Costs of medicines above the limit are shared as much as possible by individuals and their team. Outpatient visits to a doctor at the Huadong Commune Hospital are five cents for members, and hospital rooms are free except for meals. Overall, these brigade plans tend to break even financially. In 1977, the proportion of all brigades in China belonging to a cooperative medical system was reported to be 85 percent.

Mental patients live with their own team unless their condition is very serious. Only then are they referred to the Guangzhou Mental Hospital. One Huadong doctor received some psychiatric training in Guangzhou, and specialists from the city visit the commune occasionally to instruct barefoot doctors in dealing with resident mental patients. Huadong has one or two cases per brigade. Treatments include the use of medicines and *zuo tan,* "sitting and talking."

Women

Photo essays featuring model women who work in traditionally masculine jobs—jet fighter pilot, oil driller, tractor driver, scientist or cadre—appear regularly in the Chinese press. To be fully appreciated, however, this official support of women's liberation in China must be viewed in the context of its evolution.

Old China's sexual caste system differed only in detail from social codes elsewhere that allowed men to treat women, especially young married women, as property, as domestic servants, as raisers of children, and as suppliers of erotic pleasure. The code was even written down in China. The thousand-year-old *Classic for Women,* a rigid list of rules of conduct composed by disciples of Confucius, specified proper dress and behavior inside and outside the home. It mostly restricted women to the narrow family circle, depriving them of social activities. The *Classic* advocated "feet bound . . . confined within thousands of turns," a painful custom inflicted on girls starting at about age five. To form a "lily foot," wrapping bandages would be tightened gradually until the arch was broken and the toes were turned under, forming a crippling but erotically admired shape. Happily for women of Huadong Commune, this brutal practice was less prevalent in South China than in the North. Other rules of the *Classic,* however, affected northern and southern women alike. All were taught that "lack of talent is a women's virtue," that "if she's good and virtuous she's a gem in the home," and that women should be meek and submissive in everything, just as "hens are not supposed to herald the morning with their cackle.''

Chinese young people began protesting such stuffy Confucian traditions long before the Communist Party adopted the issue. Girls' schools opened early in the twentieth century, and Chinese university women first took to the streets in political demonstration in May 1919. A famous peasant uprising in 1927 included widespread demonstrations on International Working Women's Day. Marching women, wearing straw sandals in muddy town streets, thus exposing their bare feet in public—a bold act at the time—demanded that China "smash the [Confucian] man-eat-man ethical code" and called for a national women's organization. In the 1940s, women formed militia units to help resist the invading Japanese army, even though village men called them "wild women" and argued that "soldiering is men's business. Women's job is to stay home and ply the needle.''

The CCP supported the radical women's movement from very early in Party history. Mao Zedong often spoke in favor of the movement: "When women all over the country rise up, that will be the day of victory for the Chinese revolution." His support helped women overcome attitudes of deference. Peasant men, however, resented having the Party encourage their wives and daughters to "rise up." Party leaders, eager to attract support from both rural men and women, faced a difficult dilemma. They tried arguing that under the old system of class exploitation poor peasant men could not afford to have families, but to no avail. Even these "liberated" inheritors of the revolution proved extremely reluctant to give up the position of superiority over their womenfolk. Further opposition came from older women; they had suffered the low status of girlhood and early marriage themselves, and now they looked forward to enjoying the relatively higher status of age. Necessarily, the Party chose compromise and moved to contain the most militant feminist demands in an effort to avoid alienating peasant men and detracting from the struggle against landlords.

a

c

PLATE 18. *a*: Mrs. Jiang (age sixty) and her daughter-in-law (age forty). A new bride in her husband's household has little status, and may be dominated by her mother-in-law. But after bearing six children, and after her mother-in-law retires as a team laborer, the daughter-in-law may become the dominant figure. (Robert Neiderberger) *b*: A woman

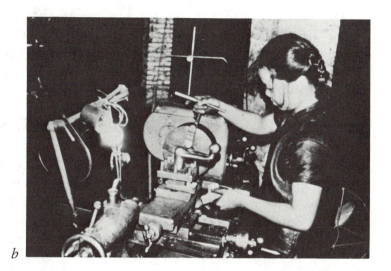

does "man's work" as a lathe operator in a commune machine shop.
(John McCoy) *c*: Arguments heard that women are better suited physio-
logically for this task may be correct. But there is no disguising the fact
that it is painful and arduous to work all day bent over at the waist.
(Robert Neiderberger) *d*: Zhang Liyi's daughter-in-law cares for her son,
after contributing a day's labor to her production team. (Andrew Nathan)

On May 1, 1950, in one of the new communist government's first pieces of legislation, a "Marriage Law" was promulgated. Among its twenty-seven articles were such points as, "Husband and wife are companions living together and shall enjoy equal status in the home" (Article 7), and "Both husband and wife shall have the right to free choice of occupation and free participation in work or in social activities" (Article 9). A vigorous campaign to popularize the new law was mounted over the next two years, but resulting tensions in some villages rose to the level of sexual warfare. Organized women violently beat recalcitrant men, and angry men beat and murdered young female activists in several instances. Unorganized women dared not claim their rights under the Marriage Law. In 1953, the Party decided to delay popularization of the law until its rural leadership had been strengthened and conditions were better.

A new stage began with the formation of people's communes in 1958. China's leaders planned to "leap forward" through labor-intensive undertakings and hoped to acquire much of the needed labor force expansion by recruiting women from rural homes. Many household tasks were collectivized to free women for new jobs with pay. Communes rapidly organized nurseries, kindergartens, commune-run dining halls, and collective enterprises such as laundries, weaving and sewing cooperatives, and shoemaking and repair shops. All this activity had a radical effect on home life but did not break down norms regarding what constituted "women's work." Their work was just collectivized. Child care, elementary and secondary teaching, nursing duties in public health and medicine, community services, and many handicrafts still were considered particularly suited to the temperament and "special responsibilities" of women. During the adjustment of the commune system in the early 1960s, family life was reemphasized. Themes of popular literature again included traditional kinship relations, filial obligations, respect for elders, and even patriarchal authority within the family. Official agitation for women's rights correspondingly declined.

Ideological stress on women's participation was renewed during the Cultural Revolution. Chairman Mao directed that "a reasonable percentage" of women should be included on all Party committees, and some communes set their proportion as high as 25 percent. By the early 1970s, however, Huadong's Party Committee included only three women (14 percent), and its Revolutionary Committee included only two women (8 percent). This type of change came slowly to Huadong. A September 1971 article in the Party's theoretical monthly, *Hongqi (Red Flag)*, included some strong language about the importance of advancing "women's work," that is, the movement to improve the status of women: "Within the ranks of the people, there still are present mistaken ideas of various sorts which belittle women and impede the coming into play of women's revolutionary strength. For this reason, to make a success of women's work is a serious class struggle as well as a battle for changing customs. . . . Party committees at various levels should put women's work on the order of the day and grasp it seriously."[21] Then a mass campaign to "criticize Confucius" began in the summer of 1973. The attacks on Confucius's teaching that girls must obey their fathers and older brothers, brides their husbands, and widows their sons added fresh momentum to the feminist cause.

This political history provides the background necessary for understanding the evolving problems of Huadong women. In the early 1970s, women made up 52 percent of the population of Huadong and were also 52 percent of the commune's labor force. They accounted for 45 percent of Huadong's students, 43 percent of the militia, 40 percent of the Communist Youth League, 34 percent of the members of competitive sports teams, and 20 percent of the membership of the CCP. The above indicates that they lagged slightly in education and lagged considerably in recruitment to elite political organizations.

Other evidence shows the continued force of tradition at Huadong. Women still do most of the uncompensated domestic chores; men rarely help with housework or child care. Men are still critical of women who "go out," preferring that their wives and daughters stay home and not mix with men in political activities. Since team meetings are held in the evening when "good" wives are home cleaning up after dinner, feeding pigs, and putting children to bed, the housekeeping syndrome reinforces nonparticipation. A household's representative at team meetings is almost always the male head of household. Nor do women usually join informal gatherings of villagers in the evenings. These predominantly male "bull sessions" are often a significant forum for discussing team affairs and political issues. The older women of the village are another source of social pressure upon young women. Older women cling to ideas of "decent behavior" that exclude social relations with men outside the family. They also discourage young women's political activity, because they believe that it encourages "indecent and immoral conduct." One side effect of this attitude is the formation of all-female work groups.

Marriages arranged through negotiations between families are largely a thing of the past. The Marriage Law requires that "marriage shall be based upon the complete willingness of the two parties," and that "neither party shall use compulsion, and no third party shall be allowed to interfere" (Article 3). It also strictly prohibits "child betrothal" and "the exaction of money or gifts in connection with marriage" (Article 2). In fact, visitors to Huadong are told that most young people these days find their own spouses, often at work. The couple may be introduced by friends or parents, but once a couple has decided to marry, parents have no veto. The reader should not underestimate the informal influence of family elders, though. Stories continue to abound from nearby communes about families who attempt to improve their status by acquiring an in-law who is a cadre or who lives closer to the city. Bride prices and dowries (or their equivalents) are still paid, and some commune members still prefer festive wedding ceremonies and feasting to the austere ones praised in the Party-sponsored media. The old practices are dying out only slowly.

By the mid-1970s, the women's rights struggle in China was focused on the issue of "equal pay for equal work." Single-minded emphasis on female cadres subsided, and indeed one of the charges leveled against Jiang Qing (Mao's wife and one of the "gang of four" purged in 1976) portrayed her as a "phony women's champion," because she believed that "when women become leaders that is their liberation." In the eyes of her critics, this idea, with its stress upon "seizing power from men and exercising dictatorship over men," harmed the desired "unity within the ranks of the revolutionary classes." The essence of the equal pay issue was outlined in 1975 by the head of a brigade-level women's association. In her brigade, each member's workpoint base rate was determined once a year. The process began with individuals stating what they thought their rate should be. "At a meeting not long ago, while two-thirds of the men confidently stated ten points, only one strong woman had the courage to bid even nine and a half. None of the other strong women dared bid over eight." At this point the Party branch interrupted the evaluation to criticize Confucius and male supremacy and, in particular, to criticize the argument that workpoint ratings should be based on physical strength alone. The men's argument was: "If women want the same base rate, they have to do just as we do in plowing, planting, digging ditches, and carrying sacks of grain." The women retorted that, first, they had never had the chance to learn those farming skills, and second, skill at all necessary jobs should be rewarded, not just skill at jobs men do best.

> First and foremost, the comparison should be on attitude toward work, on patriotic and collectivist thinking, and contribution to the collective.

136   *Society*

We took comparison of two brigade members as an example. One is the strongest man in the village. He can lift the
diesel engine off a two-wheeled tractor and is a master at
almost any farm job. The other, a woman production team
leader, can't compete with him in this, though on most jobs
she can keep up with the men. And when it comes to taking
the lead in revolutionary criticism and theoretical study, or
making arrangements for collective labor and mobilizing
people, his contribution to the collective can't compare with
hers. Everyone finally agreed that both had their strong points
and both deserved a ten-point rating.

The outcome of this struggle was that two-thirds of the men
still got ten points. Out of 136 women, 16 (12 percent) got
ten points and 40 others (29 percent) got nine points or
more. A total of 116 women (85 percent) got a higher rating
than before.[22]

As far as we can discover, similar progress has not been
made at Huadong. Mothers may still refer to their daughters
as "my little seven-and-a-half pointer," referring to the time
a few years before when seven and a half was the highest base
rate given women in many parts of China. The old physical
strength rationale will undoubtedly take years to overcome,
even for jobs that require no physical strength. That is, a
female school teacher might be paid eight and a half workpoints a day while a male teacher with identical qualifications
is paid ten points on ground that *if* the two were doing heavy
labor the man could do more; in this sense he is believed to
be *worth* more. Moreover, where physical work is involved,
a sexual division of labor is common. Some farm tasks—
weeding, hoeing, transplanting rice seedlings, collecting fertilizer and others—are mainly done by women and are
regarded as worth less inherently, because a strong man is not
needed to perform them. But women who spend their entire
working day painfully bent over at the waist transplanting
rice seedlings ridicule the argument that a man driving a
tractor works harder. Yet they are paid less than he. Finally,
women are expected to perform the vast majority of unpaid

household chores. In the morning they arrive in the fields an hour or so late, bringing breakfast to the men. In the evening they must leave an hour or so early to prepare dinner. Thus, while they work longer each day than the men, they are not credited with a "full labor day."

The feminist cause has far to go in China despite impressive accomplishments. Huadong appears to be somewhere in the rear guard of the struggle.

Education

Controversy and experimentation have marked education policy in China from the very beginning of the communist regime. Party leaders continue to pursue contradictory goals. They have desired to expand literacy and educational opportunity rapidly, yet they have been reluctant to depend upon old teachers and old texts. They want to teach practical skills needed for development rather than mere book learning and theory, but they also want to cultivate research scientists. They try to have schools act as agents of political socialization by highlighting the question, "Whom does education serve?" At the same time, however, they want students to learn academic subjects competently (the ideal is to become both "red *and* expert"). Finally, Party leaders would like to see the majority of students be children of favored social classes—workers, and poor and lower-middle peasants—rather than children of the former privileged classes. They would also like, however, to allot scarce school places to students who can learn easiest and perform best as skilled professionals after graduation. These dilemmas are still apparent in debates over educational issues, and the struggle to resolve them still results in much experimentation.

Rural schools have presented more problems than urban schools, because students are less prepared for academic achievement, fewer qualified teachers are available, and buildings are less well equipped. Education at Huadong faces

TABLE 4.1

Regular Education at Huadong Commune, 1973

Academic Level	No. of Years	No. of Schools	No. of Teachers	No. of Students	Percent Who Advance to Next Level
Primary	5	28	323	7,352	28
Junior middle	2	24*	116	2,077	58
Senior middle	3	3	53	1,215	2
University	3-4			21	
		31*	492	10,665	

*The junior middle schools were attached to primary schools.

all these problems. Before 1949, half the adult men and four-fifths of the adult women had never attended a class. Now, after a generation of the commune system, primary education has been made universal and visitors are told that literacy has reached 75 percent (see Table 4.1). By 1973, the only school-age children not enrolled were seven-year-olds whose parents believed they were still too young. Three of the twenty-one Huadong students attending a university were "sent-down youth."

A separate type of advanced training is offered by an expanding system of agricultural and technical colleges. Huadong Commune has established its own college, and a more elaborate one is found at the Hua County seat. Our Huadong visitors' reports provide few details about this institution, but similar colleges elsewhere in China are known to offer three-year majors in agronomy, orchards and forestry, water conservancy, water project construction, hydrology, and stock breeding and veterinary science. Each year, students spend several months in the classroom and several more months back working with their team. They become gradually more involved in experimentation and instruction of others in their home team. Agricultural and technical colleges also give short courses for older farmers.

The apparently contradictory goal of training students to be both "red and expert" has proven elusive. First, while reliance on entrance examinations favors smarter students—frequently those from a more privileged background—thereby discriminating against workers and poor and lower-middle peasants, reliance on pure political recommendation favors students from poorer classes and may discriminate against those from formerly more advantaged families. Consequently, both exams and recommendation have been used, sometimes in combination with geographical quotas. Second, while testing and grading in schools advances higher achieving students but holds back slower ones who are disproportionately workers and peasants, experiments with tutoring and passing everyone benefit students from deprived backgrounds but result in loss of professional quality, at least in the short run. As a result, minimal scholarly standards have become more common, although ways are still tried to help students from politically favored classes to make the grade. Third, while curriculum emphasis on textbook knowledge gives students a general foundation in a subject, very often such understanding cannot be easily put to use. Curriculum emphasis on practical knowledge trains young people to be productive as quickly as possible at a cost of producing graduates with no capacity to grow intellectually and to analyze novel problems. In recent years, while the virtues of combining theory and practice remain a firm ideal, a new back-to-basics trend is visible as well. Math, scientific knowledge, and English language training are emerging as important subjects, in addition to courses in political Marxism, revolutionary history, militia training, and physical exercise.

In the 1970s, most of Huadong's schoolhouses are basic, plain buildings. Whatever luxuries exist, such as a basketball court or a library, were probably built by the students themselves. Classroom routines often appear quite unaffected by the so-called revolution in education: pupils sitting on wooden stools behind rows of desks obediently recite rote answers. Increasingly, teachers are recruited from among the educated "down-to-the-villages youth." Some English literature is read now but is still rarely discussed. Emphasis upon political "lessons" remains the first priority. Even math problems are politicized (for example, figuring the advantage gained in the old days by a landlord who rigged his scale to cheat his tenants on the rent grain). Students spend time participating in productive labor—from the youngest primary school child who packs light bulbs into boxes to the most advanced university degree candidate who hauls rocks for a new aqueduct. They also compile local histories of their county, commune, village, and family to document differences between the "bitterness" of the old days and the "sweetness" of the new. Also, old people from the commune are invited to classrooms from time to time to give personal testimony about the miseries they suffered before the Communist Party came to power.

The typical middle school textbook for studying English is a small paperback consisting of about two dozen chapters. Each chapter contains a brief reading followed by questions and answers. The following notes by an American teacher who visited Huadong in 1974 indicate the contents of one such text used in a commune school.[23]

Chapter 1. "The East is Red" (title of the former Chinese tional anthem)

Chapter 2. "A Quotation from Chairman Mao." Part of the reading is a famous quote by Mao on education: "In industry learn from Daqing; in agriculture learn from Dazhai; the whole nation should learn from the People's Liberation Army; the Army should learn from the people of the whole country."

Chapter 3. "A Small Factory Learns from Daqing"

Chapter 4. "We Love Labor"

Chapter 5. "My Sisters"

Chapter 6. "Different Lives in Different Societies." Although it is only eight lines in length, the reading tells of a Chinese worker who has two hands, works, and is happy in contrast to an American worker who also has two hands but is out of work and is unhappy.

Chapter 7. "We Make Progress Together"

Chapter 8. "Train for the Revolution"

In sum, all the children of Huadong receive at least five years of primary education, and about half of them go on to middle school or technical courses (or both). They are taught to respect physical labor and working people. They are brought to understand China's new political values. The quality of courses in straightforward academic subjects appears to be improving every year, but future changes should be significant.

Friends and Recreation

Huadong people work hard most of the time. Many of them enjoy only one day off every two weeks. Their spare time occurs in the evening or during holidays and festivals. Some team members like to spend time off relaxing with their family, working on their private plot, or attending team meetings or classes. Still, there is time for other recreation, especially for young people, for men whose household chores are lighter than women's, and for everybody during the agricultural slack season.

The most popular team sport at Huadong is basketball (an American import), played on an outdoor court. Soccer and volleyball come in second and third. Most brigades have a court and a playing field. Competitions are popular at all levels, even among production teams, and Huadong Commune matches its best athletes against those of nearby communes. Tournaments are ordinarily held in May and October in connection with annual International Labor Day and

National Day Celebrations. Altogether Huadong has 7,565 players on 753 organized sports teams, one-third of them for women. All adult players are workers; none is a professional athlete. Only players on China's national teams train formally and take fortified diets, and even these athletes put in some time each day as ordinary workers. Other sports enjoyed in the Huadong area include pingpong, swimming, track and field events, Chinese boxing (*guoshu*, known to Westerners as kung-fu), jogging, weightlifting, hunting, and fishing.

Friends like to go off together on picnics or to visit the commune center for shopping and a restaurant meal. Those with musical talent enjoy gathering together to sing and to play the guitar or one of the traditional Chinese instruments. The more musically and dramatically talented may join the production team's performing arts troupe, or the brigade's spare-time art and literary propaganda team.

In addition to group recreation, team members also value the intimacy of close friendships and the solitude of private pursuits. Poker (rarely gambling) and Chinese chess with friends are popular pastimes, along with the monthly film shows of the commune's mobile projection team. The best times among good friends, however, may center about no particular activity at all. People who have labored hard or participated in the group life of their team may particularly enjoy whiling away a few hours talking with their friends about how their lives are going, their private yearnings, their families, their jobs and their health, about what it might be like to live in Guangzhou or even Hongkong, team and brigade affairs and personalities, and political or intellectual topics of personal interest. Friends may be of the opposite sex or of different class background, but usually they are people whose life situations are similar, who feel they have much to share with each other, and who are mutually sympathetic. Intimate friendships take a while to form, because people want to be sure that they can trust their friends never to reveal their private thoughts to others. Among students,

a

b

PLATE 19. *a*: Except in harvest season, this threshing floor doubles as an outdoor basketball court. (Andrew Nathan) *b*: Playing cards is popular at Huadong, although gambling is not. (Robert Neiderberger)

the most enduring friendships may form among classmates in middle school or higher. Often former classmates working in different places will write each other frequently and travel fairly long distances for visits when time is available. Close friendships can act as a calm haven from the encompassing pressures of collective political life. Reading, especially novels, and listening to the radio are the most common private enjoyments. Hongkong stations can be received at Huadong by those who dare to risk being caught listening to a "decadent capitalist" broadcast.

Broadly speaking, the CCP is trying to reconstitute on its own terms a social system that had been disintegrating from repeated pounding by imperial dynastic decline, confrontation with the more modern West, disunity, and war. The Communist revolution was carried forward by these earlier waves, but it also amplified them. The problem for the Party in power has been to ride the crest, to stay in command of fundamental social changes that are not completely of its making.

Suggested Reading

Population

Thomas P. Bernstein, *Up to the Mountains and Down to the Villages: The Transfer of Youth from Urban to Rural China* (New Haven, Conn.: Yale University Press, 1977).

Maurice Freedman, *Chinese Lineage and Society: Fukien and Kwangtung* (New York: Humanities Press, 1966).

Leo Orleans, *Every Fifth Child: The Population of China* (Stanford, Calif.: Stanford University Press, 1972).

Public Health and Medical Care

Joshua S. Horn, *Away With All Pests: An English Surgeon in People's China: 1954-1969* (New York: Monthly Review

Press, 1969).

Malia S. Johnson, "Prevention First: China's Road to Health," 1978 (slide show and tape available from Butterfly Productions, 810 East 32nd Street, Austin, Texas 78705).

Victor W. Sidel and Ruth Sidel, *Serve the People: Observations on Medicine in the People's Republic of China* (New York: Josiah Macy Foundation, 1974).

Women

Phyllis Andors, "Social Revolution and Woman's Emancipation: China during the Great Leap Forward," *Bulletin of Concerned Asian Scholars*, 7, no. 1 (January-March 1975): 33-40.

Kay Ann Johnson, "Women in China: Problems of Sex Inequality and Socioeconomic Change," in Joan I. Roberts, ed., *Beyond Intellectual Sexism* (New York: McKay, 1976), pp. 286-319.

Roxanne Witke and Margery Wolf, eds., *Women in Chinese Society* (Stanford, Calif.: Stanford University Press, 1975).

Marilyn Young, ed., *Women in China* (Ann Arbor: University of Michigan, Center for Chinese Studies, 1973).

Family Life

Maurice Freedman, ed., *Family and Kinship in Chinese Society* (Stanford, Calif.: Stanford University Press, 1970).

William L. Parish, Jr., and Martin King Whyte, *Village and Family in Contemporary China* (Chicago: University of Chicago Press, forthcoming).

Education

Gordon Bennett and Ronald N. Montaperto, *Red Guard: The Political Biography of Dai Siao-ai* (1971; reprint ed., Gloucester, Mass.: Peter Smith, 1977).

Jan Myrdal, *Report from a Chinese Village* (New York: Pantheon, 1965).

Susan Shirk, "The High School Experience in China" (book-length manuscript in preparation).

Friends and Recreation

Jan Myrdal, *Report from a Chinese Village* (New York: Pantheon, 1965).

Ezra Vogel, "From Friendship to Comradeship: The Change in Personal Relationships in China," *The China Quarterly*, no. 21 (January-March 1965): 46-60.

5
Culture

Chairman Mao was fond of comparing China's culture to a blank sheet of paper "which is good for writing on." China's cultural level was not very high in his opinion. This might sound like an odd comment coming from an intensely nationalistic leader of a country foreign scholars regard as having one of the richest cultural traditions in the world. Mao, however, was not referring to Shang bronzes, Tang poetry, Sung painting, and the *Dream of the Red Chamber.* He was talking about the cultural and scientific level of ordinary people who were illiterate and who had never been able to enjoy China's historical treasure chest of fine arts and letters.

The CCP's cultural policy begins with the question, "Whom should we serve?" Artists and writers are urged to emphasize political themes in the life of laboring people, not abstraction. Also, popular participation in artistic composition and performance is actively encouraged. In the sphere of customs and traditions, the Party has been iconoclastic toward "superstitions" such as expensive funerals, which it regards as wasteful and reminiscent of bourgeois or feudal culture. At the same time it has been tolerant, even supportive, of other popular customs and traditional rituals such as grave sweeping. The communists have no desire to completely abandon their Chineseness.

a

b

PLATE 20. *a*: Peasant painting from Huxian, Shaanxi Province, depicts a rural supply and marketing cooperative. The slogans to the left and right read "Develop the Economy" and "Guarantee Supplies." Displayed in the windows are bicycle parts, food items, clothing, and textiles. *b*: The wall newspaper headline commanding this Huxian peasant painting reads, "Smash the Shackles of 1000 Years; Women Can Hold Up Half the Sky." The artist depicts women in various occupational roles—laborers with ladders and spades, a postal runner with a bicycle, a lineworker with cable and tools, a tractor driver, and an older woman giving an impromptu lecture about her experiences under the old regime. *c*: This Huxian peasant painting is entitled "The Library Comes to the Fields." The artist depicts workers reading and discussing books brought to them in a cart pulled by a walking tractor.

c

Literature and Arts

Culture and politics have always mixed easily in China. What is new under the People's Republic is the participation of more people in China's cultural life. Popular culture has developed more energetically than the more professional fine arts, a trend that has gone hand in hand with greater popular participation in politics. At Huadong, commune and brigade "spare-time art and literary propaganda teams" were created in the late 1960s as part of the Great Proletarian Cultural Revolution. Individuals active in them continue to work full time in their production team, since the whole idea is to promote artistic creations that are not only popular but also politically meaningful to common laboring people with no special capacity for art appreciation.

Chinese communist thinking on the relationship between the world of culture and the world of politics goes back at least as far as Mao Zedong's 1942 "Talks at the Yenan Forum on Literature and Art," which forms one of his more remarkable statements. Mao analyzed contradictions between artistic and political criteria in literary and artistic criticism, and between popular art and elite art. He concluded that aesthetic accomplishment is desirable, but not unless the great masses of laboring people understand, appreciate, and, indeed, welcome it. Mao believed that the attitude "art for art's sake" would be harmful to the Communist Party's political task of mobilizing working-class support.

Following Mao's ideas, China's new literature and art express a strong social class bias. The subjects of paintings or sculptures and the characters of stories or plays are almost invariably workers, peasants, or soldiers, and not elite figures of ancient or modern times. The themes of literary and artistic works dignify manual labor. Man is presented as dominating nature. Optimism prevails in almost every situation; a frown or sad face is never painted except to depict revolutionary determination in the face of adversity. Works of visual art stress people over natural scenes, and the people usually appear in groups in some relationship of cooperation or unity. Action prevails over passivity; no longer does an artist portray a lonely, contemplative individual, dwarfed by a mountain paradise, lost in thought. Women receive as much attention as men, and "national minorities" (Tibetans, Muslims, Mongolians, and others) receive as much attention as Han Chinese. Fantastic or escapist themes are absent. Within the limits of the new rules, however, many traditional techniques are acceptable and even encouraged (forms of lyric poetry, use of empty space in painting, falsetto singing styles in opera, age-old humorous devices, and so on).

Many productions of Huadong's spare-time art and literary propaganda teams would probably earn low marks from Western audiences. Not only would such audiences be slow to appreciate the Chinese amateur theatrical efforts to combine cultural and political creativity; they would be insensitive as well to interesting variations on standard themes. Just as Chinese listening to jazz for the first time might too easily conclude that all twelve-bar blues sound alike—same cadence, same chord progressions, and same flatted third and seventh "blue notes," and so on—so foreigners new to Chinese drama might too hastily conclude that all revolutionary plays have the same general plot. Foreign visitors treated to successive productions by different propaganda teams might be entertained the first evening with a performance of *Think of the Consumer When Growing Vegetables.* While this might initially arouse the visitor's amused interest, the second night's performance of *Drying Grain to Store in Preparation for War* would probably be less well received. *Fitting the Bearings,* the third night's dance program about a machine shop routine, might begin to pall despite the rolling ball bearings realistically evoked by dancers' cartwheels. Most foreigners would be oblivious to fine points of the performances that regularly fascinate Chinese audiences, such as the subtly exaggerated characterization of an "activist" whose behavior borders on "opportunism," or the amusing resemblance between a character in the drama and a real person in the locality.

These propaganda teams operate wholly differently from amateur theatrical troupes familiar to Western audiences. Following each show team members invite comments and criticisms from their audience. They try to correct all inaccuracies revealed and to make needed revisions and additions if their intended message remains unclear. They even solicit original scripts for skits. Ideas contributed by brigade members with no dramatic experience may be very crude at first, but the team's approach is to help peasant playwrights rework their inspirations into usable scripts—if not for public performance then for drama practice in brigade schools. The key is to encourage, not to discourage, mass participation in cultural-political life. Similarly, brigade members' artistic and craft skills are fostered, and peasant creations that prove popular are given wider recognition. Selections of the finest peasant works are reproduced in great numbers and sold at bookstores throughout the country.

Documentary and dramatic films are displayed nightly at the Huadong Commune cinema. A mobile projection team takes some of these films "on the road," showing them from village to village around the commune on improvised outdoor screens. From time to time visiting propaganda teams from nearby People's Liberation Army units give cultural performances in Huadong's villages. Always, entertainment, education, and politics are combined.

Customs and Traditions

From the official viewpoint of the Chinese Communist Party, all old customs and traditions fall into one of two categories—feudal superstitions or "rich cultural traditions." "Superstitions" interfere with the Party's policies regarding social transformation, while other customs make up the rich cultural tradition of the Chinese people. Generally speaking, "superstitions" are bad in CCP eyes because they lead peasant households to wasteful expenditures of money, hamper the introduction of new technology in villages, are associated with proscribed organizations from precommunist society (including Buddhist and Confucian temples and missionary-established Christian churches), treat women as chattels, or reinforce the attitude that thinkers and elites have more status than physical laborers. By contrast, rich cultural traditions are good in CCP eyes because they help the Party win support from people who are very fond of many of their old customs. Policies toward China's "national minorities" are an important example of the contradiction obvious here. China's non-Han ethnic minorities total only 6 percent of the population, but they inhabit 60 percent of the country, including the sensitive border regions adjacent to the Soviet Union, Mongolia, India, Nepal, Burma, Laos, and Vietnam. China's desire for social reform in these sensitive regions, and for their assimilation into the Chinese nation, conflict with its desire to win these minority peoples' loyalty and support. Hence, Chinese minority policy has been to struggle against unacceptable "feudal" customs in those areas, such as the secular powers of the Tibetan Buddhist *lama* ("superior one") hierarchy, while actively encouraging the preservation of other elements of minority culture. The National Minorities Institute in Beijing is the organizational vehicle for this strategy. The Communist Party draws a sharp line between "superstition" and "culture," and it campaigns hard to eradicate the former. Success is greatest among young people, and in particular among young people who aspire to Party membership, higher education, or selection for training as a technician or "barefoot doctor." These aspiring, upwardly mobile youth must be willing to abandon superstitious customs and to dedicate themselves to the Party's new social values. Among the people of Huadong as a whole, however, many "superstitions" persist despite all efforts to eradicate them.

One popular effort to foster new, socialist values takes the form of stories for telling and retelling in schools and adult study groups. These stories are disseminated through newspapers and literary magazines, and versions are sold in bookstores as easily affordable thin paperbacks or even comic books. Free copies of many of them are available in brigade reading rooms or school libraries. In one story an old peasant woman's relatives lay plans to honor her on her birthday. When she returns from work that day, they enthusiastically unveil their surprise, a celebration and games they have arranged. But the old woman shocks them by refusing to participate in the merriment and walks off angrily from the house. Before long she reappears with a handful of herbs, which she proceeds to boil into bitter tea to serve to all the relatives. The bitter taste of the herbs, she says, should remind them of life in the old days and of how different it was from the sweetness of commune life now. This woman's haughty behavior might seem sanctimonious and insulting, and we might regard any real person who acted in this way as rather arrogant. But just such an emotional effect on listeners is intended by storytellers, who exaggerate dramatically the frivolity of the relatives and sternness of the old woman's response. With their listeners' attention fixed, they can transmit the moral of the story all the more persuasively.

In past generations, one enormous pressure on rural family finances was the marriage of a son or daughter. Years of savings might be squandered on this all-important event in their lives, and many families would be willing to go deeply into debt to give a proper wedding. Expenses included the cost of a wedding feast, gifts, and sometimes a bride price or dowry. In Huadong Commune today, by contrast, policy is to encourage extremely simple and frugal marriages. Compliance with the policy is far from complete, but wedding feasts, if they occur at all, are far more modest than in the past, and gifts (limited by the selection available on local markets) are relatively inexpensive practical items. We have no firm data on the practice of paying bride prices and dowries among Huadong families, only the knowledge that it still exists in nearby villages. Families who wish to withdraw a substantial proportion of their savings all at once are questioned by the comrades of Huadong Commune's branch of the People's Bank or of a brigade Credit Cooperative office. These banking officials may not prevent a family from making a withdrawal because the anticipated expenditure violates Party policy, but they do make efforts at persuasion and sometimes they manage compromises. More subtly, we can easily imagine a situation in which some members of a family appreciate being able to use the external "discipline" of the banking comrades as an argument against traditional grandparents or others insisting upon more lavish festive outlays.

Another enormous pressure on family savings or indebtedness used to be the cost of funerals, especially in the case of well-to-do families for whom the size of a funeral was a conspicuous indicator of social position. Relatives and friends used to participate in elaborate funeral ceremonies.

Now a simple memorial service is held. The departed used to be dressed in fine clothing and laid to rest in an all-wooden coffin, if the family could afford it. Now the body is dressed in everyday clothing and placed in a wooden frame casket with straw mat sides. This not only costs the family less but also saves on scarce lumber. Mourners, often strangers who were paid simply to swell the retinue, used to dress in special funeral costume and march in a public procession. Various items would be ceremonially burned for the spirit of the deceased to enjoy in the next world—food and gold-colored paper "money" at the least, and (for wealthier families) impressively crafted paper cars and houses, often with servants. Now mourners merely wear armbands or borders sewn on sleeves to symbolize their grief. Bereaved families used to consult a geomancer, or specialist in the spirit world, who it was believed could determine the most favorable place for a gravesite. Unhappily, the "best site" would sometimes turn out to be on fertile cropland, and graves would be placed there despite interference with plowing or reduction of plot size. Now caskets are buried deep or on a hillside away from producing fields, and the site indicated with a roadside marker rather than a gravestone on the spot. Thus plowing need not disturb graves, and grave mounds and markers no longer need interfere with farm work. Huadong officials have told visitors that cremation is common nowadays, but emigrés from Guangdong generally report that burial, and even "second burial" (the ritual disinterment of bones at an auspicious time), are still almost universal.

We have no specific information on the current status of many popular customs, such as fortune telling and consultations with spirit mediums, but since grave sweeping (at Qing Ming Festival) and certain popular forms of gambling (especially *shisan zhang,* or "thirteen cards") still go on, we assume that to some extent other "superstitions" also continue.

Festivals

The major festivals of old China still observed today in the Huadong area are:

Festival	Lunar Calendar	Gregorian Calendar
Lunar New Year (Spring Festival)	From the 16th day of the last month of the old year through the 15th day of the new year	The first day of the lunar new year falls between January 20 and February 20
Qing Ming (Grave Sweeping Festival)	(Established by a very complicated formula)	Usually first week in April
Duan Wu Jie (Dragon Boat Festival)	5th day of the 5th month	Late May or early June
Mid-Autumn Festival	15th day of the 8th month	September
Dong Jie (Winter Festival)	21st day of the 12th month	Late January

For the most part these traditional festivals are celebrated less elaborately now than in the past, but the essential ingredients remain—family gathering and feasting, typically with seasonal delicacies. The communists' approach to China's traditional celebrations has been to retain the more popular festivals while eliminating their religious content and the wasteful spending practices associated with them. Traditional festival days break normal work routines, allow rest, and provide occasions for dramatic or musical performances. They give people the feeling that life is more varied and enjoyable. It would be crass to equate modern CCP leaders with ancient

Roman rulers whose governing formula was to pacify the populace with "bread and circuses." Today's Communist Party leaders do not simply appeal to the multitudes; they want to educate citizens and reform culture. Yet, like their Roman counterparts, they appreciate that the people of rural China love festivals. Except where celebrations blatantly clash with the Party's progressive ideas, leaders not only tolerate festive practices that have attracted popular enthusiasm for ages, they actively encourage them.

Spring Festival is a good example. No other holiday is more welcome to the people of Huadong. All schooling and work comes to a halt. Preparations begin well in advance. The supply and marketing cooperative lays in stocks of new clothes, bright red paper for writing New Year's greetings, seasonal sweets, extra pork (if available), and all the makings for stuffed dumplings (*jiaozi*). Family members who are separated arrange to reunite: children away at school return home, and workers assigned to distant places take leave to visit for a few days with their parents, wives, and children. Even Red Guards used to return to their native villages for Spring Festival during the height of the Cultural Revolution. Beforehand, a brief political campaign is coupled with small-group study to remind people of the need for frugality in feasting and gift giving during the holiday season and to underscore official warnings against gambling, incense burning, exploding strings of firecrackers late at night, and "kowtowing" (children used to have to *ketou,* or touch their heads to the ground, before their elders).

The holiday now lasts only three days instead of the traditional two weeks or more, and some activists even make a display of returning to the fields after relaxing only two days. For most people, however, the pace of life naturally slows during this slack time in the farming cycle; projects such as waterworks or road construction are suspended. Many changes have occurred from the old days. Men and boys participate less often in parades and dragon dances, gambling is reduced to a minimum, and drinking bouts have all but disappeared. Fewer women burn offerings to household deities or cook elaborate meals to offer to ancestors before they are eaten by the family. *Hongbao* (red envelopes) containing "lucky money" for children are seldom exchanged, and gift giving is limited to family members, whereas before many friends would bring presents too. Bright red *duilian,* or paper strips with New Year's greetings inscribed in black characters, are still pasted beside doorways; but old inscriptions about achieving wealth and good fortune have given way to new ones like "Serve the People" or "Long Live the People's Communes." No longer is a new picture of the kitchen god placed above the stove; Zao Wang has given way to a portrait of the late Chairman Mao Zedong, or perhaps to new Chairman Hua Guofeng. Visitors to each house are still greeted with *longans,* lychees, and sweets, and festive performances by spare-time art and literary propaganda teams are well attended. One skit inevitably reaffirms the benefits of working together closely during the spring plowing and planting season soon to follow.

Qing Ming (literally "clear and bright," one of the twenty-four terms used commonly in agricultural communities to describe the days on which characteristically seasonal weather begins) follows Chun Fen (vernal equinox) and precedes Gu Yu (grain rains) each spring. Originally, Qing Ming was the day when families went to the burial sites of their ancestors, repaired the graves, offered a feast to the spirits of the departed, and held a memorial service. It is also a popular time for walks in the fields or picnics in the country, as most flowers and trees are in bloom. Gourds used to be planted on this day as a superstitious protection against injury by insects. Local authorities in Guangdong Province still acknowledge this traditional holiday by allowing overseas Chinese from Hongkong, Macao, and elsewhere to cross the border and return home to tend their ancestors' graves (and visit their families). Many additional people must be mobilized for "public security" work during this period to keep an eye out for Nationalist Chinese agents mixed in among the throngs of people who take advantage of the opportunity for temporary visas to enter the People's Republic. Thus, one benefit of Qing Ming at Huadong is to allow family reunions with relatives from Hongkong or abroad.

The major new holidays introduced by the Communist Party are:

> New Year—January 1
> International Working Women's Day—March 8
> International Labor Day—May 1
> Youth Day—May 4
> Children's Day—June 1
> Anniversary of the Founding of the CCP (1921)—July 1
> Anniversary of the Founding of the People's
>   Liberation Army (1927)—August 1
> National Day (People's Republic of China
>   proclaimed, 1949)—October 1

The new holidays honor various social sectors for their revolutionary contributions. Women's Day features lectures, films, and cultural presentations depicting the new status of women in the People's Republic. International Labor Day celebrates the cause of working classes throughout the world. It also is an occasion for one of the two most important sports meets each year (the other being National Day). Youth Day commemorates the famous "May Fourth" demonstration of 1919, when students from Beijing University took to the streets of the capital to protest decisions of the Versailles Conference unfavorable to China. This day was a great moment in the history of modern Chinese nationalism, and the present government is eager to have today's youth understand its significance. Children's Day features performances and arts and crafts exhibitions by younger children.

Party Day and Army Day are rather straightforward political affairs. National Day, with a combination of political and cultural events, fetes the anniversary of the establishment

FIGURE 5.1 **ANNUAL CYCLE AND CALENDAR OF HOLIDAYS**

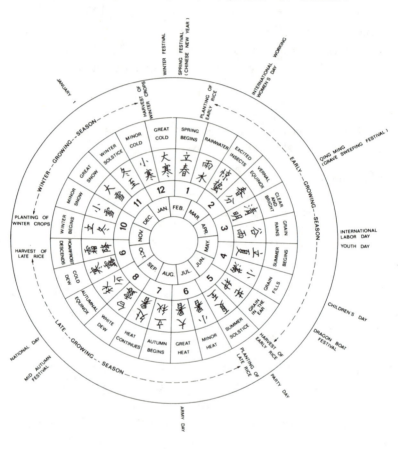

of the People's Republic. At Huadong, as elsewhere, teams from production teams and brigades compete in basketball, pingpong, swimming, and track and field events, the winners advancing to competitions as high as the province level. Still, the richest festivals in the minds of rural villagers are the traditional ones.

Several lesser festivals and celebrations, most of them traditional, add further color to commune life.

Suggested Reading

Literature and Arts

John Berninghausen and Ted Huters, eds., *Revolutionary Literature in China: An Anthology* (White Plains, N.Y.: M.E. Sharpe, 1976).

W. J. F. Jenner, ed., *Modern Chinese Stories* (New York: Oxford University Press, 1970).

Colin Mackerras, *Amateur Theater in China 1949-1966*, Contemporary China Paper, no. 5 (Canberra: Australian National University Press, 1973).

Walter Meserve and Ruth I. Meserve, eds., *Modern Drama from Communist China* (New York: New York University Press, 1970).

Mary Sheridan, "The Emulation of Heroes," *China Quarterly*, no. 33 (January-March 1968): 47-72.

Customs and Traditions

William L. Parish, Jr., and Martin King Whyte, *Family and Village in Contemporary China* (Chicago: University of Chicago Press, forthcoming).

Max Weber, *The Religion of China*, trans. H. H. Gerth (Glencoe, Ill.: Free Press, 1951).

Arthur Wolf, ed., *Religion and Ritual in Chinese Society* (Stanford, Calif.: Stanford University Press, 1975).

C. K. Yang, *Religion in Chinese Society* (Berkeley and Los Angeles: University of California Press, 1961).

See also Gary Seaman's catalog, *Films on the Culture and Society of Traditional China*. Much of the information in this fine series of documentaries on Chinese popular religion is not available in published sources. For a catalog, write to Far Eastern Audio Visuals, P.O. Box 543, Cedar Park, TX 78613.

Festivals

Jack Chen, *A Year in Upper Felicity: Life in a Chinese Village during the Cultural Revolution* (New York: Macmillan, 1973).

6
The 1980s and Beyond

The preceding chapters have sought to piece together Huadong's story with three goals in mind—to be comprehensive, to introduce a personal perspective wherever possible, and to highlight change. They have touched on all aspects of commune life from Communist Party leadership to festivals in order to impart a sense of Huadong as an integrated community and not just as an economic unit. In presenting what is known about Huadong, we have also put forward informed surmises as to how people living there might feel about and evaluate commune policies. We are the least confident about this part of our effort, even though each of our conjectures has some factual basis, for popular attitudes and values remain one of the least well understood aspects of contemporary Chinese society. Finally, we have stressed key changes in commune organization and routine, from the tumult of the Great Leap Forward to the relative calm of the 1970s. The question now regards what lies ahead. Is it possible to foresee the general directions of further change?

The readjustment of the early communes was codified in the sixty-article "Regulations on the Work of the Rural People's Communes (Revised Draft)" passed by the CCP Central Committee on September 27, 1962.[24] They are still in force, as far as we know. Although these regulations remain in draft form, and have never been published officially, they embody one of the few important policies that survived the Cultural Revolution unscathed. For the most part, the size, ownership, work organization, financing, and management of today's communes remain the same as in 1962. The regulations contain a promise that no further basic changes would be made for at least thirty years (until 1992).[25]

The collective principle is secure. The state gives no signs of eagerness to nationalize agriculture and make it a public enterprise. Nor are voices heard today supporting revival of "responsibility systems" or other policies that would expand the private sector. Small private plots along with limited free markets should continue to exist as before in a dominant environment of collective ownership, enterprises, incentives, and welfare.

The three-level system of ownership will probably change only slowly. Many communes have tried to move the basic unit of ownership and accounting up from the team level to the brigade level, eliminating the need for teams in the process. We can look forward to further consolidation of production brigades only where local conditions are favorable. Production teams should survive for two or three decades or more.

Rural small-scale industries appear to have a bright future. They make good economic sense for large, agricultural countries like China, however inefficient they might be for wealthier, more industrialized economies. For one thing, transportation is expensive in China, and deliveries of major equipment like farm machinery may be delayed in any case if orders have not been incorporated into existing factory production plans. For another thing, unexploited local resources often are available at reasonable cost, and small plants near customers can know their customers' needs more easily and can serve them better than distant factories. Also, industrialization of the countryside narrows the urban-rural gap, and rural small-scale industries help introduce modern technology to the countryside more quickly than large urban plants can. In short, rural small-scale industry gives more effective support for agriculture than does larger industry in cities.

We expect the present modest standard of living and basic commitment to relative egalitarianism to change only slowly, unless China's material prosperity unexpectedly surges ahead of population growth. More consumer goods should gradually come onto the market, but many years are likely to pass before the familiar stress on frugality and on a plain and simple lifestyle disappear from Chinese rhetoric.

"Self-reliance" should survive as a primary value. This concept expresses the opposite of dependence in both domestic and foreign affairs. At home, it discourages dependence on state aid, while abroad it abhors dependence on foreign powers and on unpredictable international markets. In neither case is it likely to be equated with autarky; it will stress the importance of "keeping the initiative in our own hands," in Chairman Mao's phrase.

Finally, we expect community improvement to continue along present lines. More barefoot doctors will be trained, more facilities will be acquired by rural clinics, and more rural people will be covered by cooperative medical plans. The quality of commune schools should improve, and more agricultural and technical courses should be offered. Opportunities for amateur cultural participation should grow in scope and improve in quality.

Other changes are more difficult to plot. Population growth might level off to a maximum of 1 percent per year by 1990, and perhaps even to zero thereafter. Better quality education in commune schools, coupled with more immigration of educated city youth, should create a larger pool of capable leadership and technical expertise in the countryside. The new official dedication to farm mechanization and modernization under Chairman Hua Guofeng should bring dramatic improvements to places that can swiftly absorb new technology. Revolutionary committees may revert to "people's committees," a form common before the Cultural Revolution.

In straightforward economic terms, China's rural achievement since the 1950s has been impressive and the commune system has been instrumental to much of that achievement. Even if the critical statistic of "per capita grain output" has increased or decreased only slightly, depending upon whose estimates are used, there is little doubt that in many other ways the quality of life in China's countryside has improved significantly since villages and farms were reorganized into teams, brigades, and communes. The question for the future is whether or not this record can be sustained.

Huadong is a good case in point. Most reclaimable new land has already been reclaimed and brought into production. Little underutilized labor power exists at Huadong, so only small new contributions are expected from that sector. Most of the possible addition to agricultural productivity from new irrigation and flood control projects has already occurred. The "New Liuqi" canal, the Jiuwantan reservoir, the Liqi dam, and other construction have brought 96 percent of Huadong's cultivated acreage under gravity-feed irrigation. The most pronounced effect of agricultural mechanization is an increase in the cropping index, that is, a rise in the proportion of cultivatable acreage that can be double-cropped or triple-cropped. But Huadong already triple crops 80 percent of its cropland from January through May, 90 percent from May through November, and 45 percent from November through January. Hence little further improvement is possible. Higher chemical fertilizer application increases "yield response" (the incremental rise in crop yield due to an increment of fertilizer) only up to a point; thereafter, greater fertilizer application results in smaller increases. A leading expert on Chinese agriculture, economist Dwight Perkins, estimates that "in some rice growing regions, the rate of application [of nutrients] is 150 kilograms per hectare or more. At such levels one would expect yield response to be falling.[26] Calculating from the figures presented in Chapter 3 under the heading "Grain Farming," more than 160 kilograms of "nutrients" (both organic and chemical fertilizers) are applied per hectare at Huadong. Thus, Perkins would would probably estimate that the yield response at Huadong is falling and would continue to do so, even if greater amounts of chemical fertilizer could be economically absorbed. Grain imports are another way to raise per-capita food consumption. In the late 1970s, however, China is importing on the average an amount of grain equivalent to one-half kilogram (about one pound) per person per month, that is, not very much. Imports seem to have more of an impact upon a few priority regions than they do upon China as a whole, and they seem to be more related to farm incentives than to necessary food supply.[27]

The terms of urban-rural trade (the ratio of farm prices to prices farmers must pay for manufactures) are still improving. Also, the agricultural tax, fixed at an absolute amount in 1952-1953, continues to decline in proportion to the whole of each successive crop. Economist Perkins, assessing the total transfer of resources out of agriculture into industry, the military, and other uses, concludes that two points are reasonably clear:

> On the one hand, there continues to be some net drain of resources away from agriculture to other uses. On the other hand, the drain has certainly declined when expressed as a percentage of farm income measured in current prices. There may even have been a significant reduction in this net drain in absolute terms as well. Whatever the precise figure, there is little doubt that the often stated shift in priorities implied by the term "take agriculture as the foundation" is reflected in substantial changes in the proportion of real resources flowing to and from agriculture.[28]

The final factor is new technology, in particular new and more abundant seed strains. Scientific advances could have a big impact on farm production, but so far the most dramatic progress has been made with wheat, not rice. Much of what commune authorities could do to raise rice yield at Huadong may have been done already. Thus, the greatest improvements in the quality of life there are likely to occur in other ways—e.g., via the lightening of farm labor through electrification and mechanization, the shift of employment to industrial production, the promotion of more variety in diets, the proliferation of social services, and the expansion of educational opportunities.

Appendix A

Summary Chronology

1949–1957
Liberation,
Land Reform, and
Agricultural
Collectivization

Year	China	Guangdong Province	Huadong Commune
1949	People's Republic of China proclaimed (October 1)	Liberation of Guangzhou City (October 13)	
1950	Marriage law promulgated (May 1)		
1952		Tao Zhu becomes prominent CCP leader in the province	
1953		Mutual aid teams (of six or more households) organized	
1954	State Constitution adopted (September 20)	Elementary agricultural producers' cooperatives (APCs) organized	
1956	Eighth CCP Congress (September)	Advanced APCs organized	
1957	Antirightist campaign (June–December)		

	China	Guangdong Province	Huadong Commune
1958-1960 Great Leap Forward			
1958	Decision to amalgamate APCs (spring)		Commune coal mine opened
	New general line for socialist construction and new strategy for the Great Leap Forward (May)		
	Decision to form communes (August 29)		Huadong People's Commune organized from about 50 advanced APCs (October)
	CCP Central Committee passes first resolutions critical of communes (December)		
1959	"Three difficult years" of bad weather begin	"Tidying up the communes" movement (spring)	Major water conservancy campaign
	CCP Central Committee decides on three-level system of ownership in communes, with the brigade as the basic level (August)		"New Liuqi" Canal constructed
			Farm tools factory constructed
			Building materials factory constructed
			Agricultural Research Center opened
1960	People's Daily announces further decentralization of communes to make the team the basic level (November)	Temporary effort begins to form communes in cities (February)	Major water conservancy campaign.

1961-1965
Recovery and
Adjustment

1961   CCP Central Committee's
"60 Articles on
Agriculture" establish
commune policy for at
least two decades (May)

1962   After the "three difficult
years," the economy begins
to revive

Socialist Education
Campaign (1962-66) launched

Truck fleet organized

Farm machinery repair
workshop constructed

CCP Central-South Bureau
leader Tao Zhu begins to
promote Huadong as an
advanced experience for
popularizing individual
incentives in agriculture
(summer)

Tao Zhu's first visit to
Huadong (October)

At the Conghua conference,
Tao Zhu designates Huadong
as a "keypoint" for intro-
ducing the "responsibility
system" (October 19)

Anna Louise Strong Visit

	China	Guangdong Province	Huadong Commune
1963	Economy almost recovers to pre-Great Leap levels		Stone quarry begins operation
			Multipurpose food processing mill constructed
			Responsibility system extended to all 20 Huadong brigades. Huadong "keypoint" widely publicized. Tao Zhu solicits contributions to insure the success of his experiment.
1964			Major water conservancy campaign
			Jiuwantan reservoir completed
			State forest established within Huadong territory
			Problems with the responsibility system become noticeable
			Derek Davies's Visit
1965	Escalation of U.S. intervention in Vietnam		Operation room added to commune hospital
	Mao's instruction, "in medical and health work put the stress on rural areas" (June)		
1966-1969 Great Proletarian Cultural Revolution			
1966	Tao Zhu promoted to Beijing as Director of the CCP Central Committee's Propaganda Department (July)		Oil processing mill constructed

1967	Tao Zhu listed as fourth ranking central CCP leader (August) Red Guards organized (August) Tao Zhu disappears, a victim of Cultural Revolution criticism (December) Year of violence among mass organizations, sometimes involving army units	Rebel mass organizations seize power from the CCP provincial committee (January 21) Military control over the province proclaimed (March 15)	Commune's first surgeon arrives from Guangzhou Mass campaign to criticize mistakes of leading cadres
1968	Order slowly restored Beginning of massive campaign to resettle urban youths in the countryside	Guangdong Province Revolutionary Committee formed (February 21)	Brigade cooperative medical plans organized "Spare-time art and literary propaganda teams" organized Dazhai workpoint system popularized
1969	Ninth CCP Congress (April)		Major water conservancy campaign Prefabricated cement products plant constructed

1970-1975 Aftermath of Cultural Revolution	China	Guangdong Province	Huadong Commune
1970			Irrigation barrage completed
			No. 1 silicon sand mine opened
			Sugar mill begins operation
			"Barefoot doctor" training classes begin
			General health checkup, including TB check
			Dazhai workpoint system begins to give way to task rates and time rates again
1971	U. S. pingpong team invited to play in China (April)		Committee of Concerned Asian Scholars Visit (June 24)
	Henry Kissinger's secret visit (July)		
1972	President Nixon's visit (February)		Jiuwantan hydroelectric power station completed
			No. 2 silicon sand mine opened
1973	Two-year campaign to "criticize Confucius" begins (summer)		Each brigade has three or four "barefoot doctors"
	Tenth CCP Congress (August)		New York State Educators' Study Group Visit (July 22-24)

1974		Claude Aubert Visit (March)
1975		U.S. Water Resources Delegation Visit (August 21)
1976– Post Mao Era		
1976	Death of Premier Zhou Enlai (January) Death of Chairman Mao (September) Purge of the "gang of four," indicating the end of some Cultural Revolution policies	
1977	Eleventh CCP Congress (August)	Elisabeth Croll Visit (April)
1978	Fifth National People's Congress (February–March)	

Appendix B

Summary of Activities of Three Levels of Ownership at Huadong People's Commune (1973)

Activity	Commune level	Brigade level	Team level
Earlier social organization corresponding to present-day collective organization	2 xiang (Tuiguang & Beixia)		
	About 50 Advanced APCs (reports vary), averaging 200 families each	2-3 Advanced APCs. Elsewhere in China brigades and Advanced APCs are equivalent in size.	
	About 200 Elementary APCs averaging 50 families each.		Most teams are significantly smaller than the Elementary APCs had been.
	Probably 4 or more standard periodic markets	Several villages (Lirong Brigade contains more than 20 villages)	1 or more villages (2-3 are common). Many teams are composed of single surname villages, or "clans"
Communist Party Leadership	1144 Party members in 1973 (women make up 20% of the Party members, but 40% of the Communist Youth League members)		
	42 Party branches in brigades, enterprises, & other organizations		
	Commune Party Congress (450 delegates, of which 150 also are delegates to the Hua County Party Congress, 19 to the Guangzhou Municipal Party Congress, and 6 to the Guangdong Province Party Congress)		

*Indicates information is from neighboring communes, not from Huadong specifically.

	Commune	Brigade	Team
	Party Committee: 21 members elected by the Congress. Meets about once every 2 months	Party branch. Meets about once a month. Most branches have 20-30 members.	Party small group (if the team has 3 or more Party members). Meets about once a week.
	Party Committee Standing Committee: 7 members (3 of them women) elected by the Party Committee. Meets once a week. Six also are members of the Commune Revolutionary Committee Standing Committee.		
	Party Secretary and 2 Deputy Secretaries elected by the Standing Committee.	Party branch secretary elected by the Committee	
	*Party Departments: Political Organization Propaganda Youth Women Military	*Party Departments: Political Organization Propaganda Youth Women Study	
Administration	Commune Assembly (430 members elected each year by brigade assemblies)	Brigade Assembly. Liirong Brigade's Assembly has 100 delegates, about 8 from each of its 12 teams	Team Assembly of all members of the team. May meet several times each month.
	Revolutionary Committee (RC): 25 members (2 of them women) elected by the Assembly. 21 are Party members, the other 4 being "mass representatives" (2 peasants, 1 worker & 1 intellectual). 2 are women. Meets about once a month, sometimes in enlarged sessions of 40-50 with invited commune members	*Revolutionary Committee: Brigade leader Dep. brigade leader Political education officer Custodian of the granary Accountant Cashier Tractor driver/repairman Custodian of equipment Women's work leader Militia leader	Team cadres: Team leader Dep. team leader Political instructor Warehouse keeper Accountant Workpoint recorder Women's work leader Militia leader *Equipment caretaker *Animal caretaker

(Meetings of all brigade members are held a few times each year to discuss brigade affairs, new mass movements, and new policies.)

Teams are subdivided into "work groups" (zu). Some are permanent and some are temporary.

Leading cadres work almost full time in the fields

RC Standing Committee: 11 members elected by RC. All are Party members. Meets about once a week. Members:
RC Chairman
Deputy chairmen for:
Industry & agriculture
Finance and trade
Political education
Culture, education, &
Public health
Responsible persons for:
Industry
Agriculture
Animal husbandry
Women's work
Militia affairs
Public security

No cadres serve full time. All cadres are expected to contribute 132 days of manual labor each year.

58 cadres are full-time administrators; 46 are former xiang officials still paid by the state, and 12 are new officials paid from collective funds. All are expected to contribute 60 days of manual labor each year.

Agricultural Tax Bureau, Industrial Bureau, Mine Office, and others are outside agencies with offices at Huadong

	Commune	Brigade	Team
Enterprises	All 11 members of the Commune RC Standing Committee serve full time. The other 14 RC members serve part time.	Altogether 45 small-scale enterprises in 1973, including:	Crops (triple-cropping area):
	Coal mine (1958)--88 employees	Farm tool shop	Paddy rice, early crop (harvested from 72% of Huadong's 12,000 cultivated acres)
	Building construction team (1958)--34	Brick, tile & lime kiln	Paddy rice, late crop (harvested from 82%)
	Building materials factory (1959)--90	Sapling nursery & forests	Barley (42%) /One recent report gives winter wheat (35%). This is being newly tried in South China./
	Farm implements factory (1959)-152	Fodder processing shop	Maize & peas (est. 5%)
	Commune farm (1959): ponds, hatcheries & orchards--43	Orchards	Peanuts, early crop (5%)
	Truck fleet, 8 vehicles in 1974 (1962)--18	Fishponds	Peanuts, late crop (9%)
	Farm machinery repair shop (1962)--53	Timber Mill	Sugar cane (1%)
	Stone quarry (1963)--32	Peanut oil pressing mill (5 altogether)	Hemp, Tobacco, Vegetables (4%)
	Multipurpose food processing mill (1963)--47	Rice mill (15 altogether)	Household private plots (4%)
	Oil processing mill (1966)--53	Coal mine (12 altogether)	
	Cement prefabricated products plant (1969)--31		Sidelines:
	Sugar mill (1970)--40		Brick, tile & lime kiln
	Silicon sand mine No. 1 (1970)--84		Pottery (bowls, vases, teapots, water pipes, porcelain insulators)
	Silicon sand mine No. 2 (1972)--72		Many others

185

Jiuwantan hydroelectric
station (1972)--20

Percent of 1972 gross income
earned by farming & industrial
enterprises at each level: 13%
(100% = 13,800,000 yuan, or
approximately $7.5 million).

	6%	81%

Producers' goods owned, including machines	11 48-hp tractors, 11 35-hp tractors, and 2 28-hp tractors.
Tractors	Altogether 200 10 to 12-hp "walking tractors" (less than 1 per team)
Tractor-drawn farm equipment	Altogether 250 power cultivators (11 to 12-hp), all-purpose machines often used simply for hauling (less than 1 per team)
Insecticide sprayers	Altogether 4,000 water buffalo (12-13 per team). Roughly half of Huadong's cultivation is by buffalo, and each buffalo gives 2 tons of manure a year.
Electric pumps	Altogether approximately 60,000-70,000 pigs, an average of more than one per person. Some are raised by household. Each pig gives 1 ton of manure a year.
Electric pumps	
Transplanters	
	No. 11 team of Linong Brigade owns:

Commune	Brigade	Team
		1 "walking tractor"
		4 threshing machines
		2 crushers
		1 potato cutting machine
		1 electric blower to separate food grain kernels from chaff
		Small hydroelectric power turbine for illumination of homes
Economic services that support teams		
Waterworks construction:		
26 reservoirs (to control drought in northern hills)		
2 dams on Liuqi River, and 4 power-pumped drainage stations (to control flooding in southern lowlands)		
Digging of 15 miles of the 75-mile "New Liuqi" Canal		
Huadong participates with 7 nearby communes (Huashan, Dongfanghong, Xinhua, Shihua, Jiangcun, Qianjin, Xiangyang) and with the "Guangzhou Municipal Liqi Irrigation District".		
Granary	Granary	Granary
Tractor & agricultural machinery repair and training of brigade & team repairmen and drivers	Agricultural machinery service	

Strong political leadership to urge teams to accept electrification, mechanization, and other innovations (chemical fertilizer, etc.).

Agricultural research & extension:

27 technical workers   Altogether, 51 technical workers (2-3 per brigade)

Agricultural Research Center (1959):   Agricultural Research Station

  Seed breeding

  Experimentation & testing of new crops

  Agronomic experimentation (e.g. optimal application of manure & fertilizer, water & insecticides, transplanting procedures)

  Maintenance of weather records

10 acres of experimental plots; 1,100 acres of designated "demonstration plots" throughout the commune   Altogether, 13 acres of experimental & seed-breeding plots

Banking and finance

Branch, People's Bank of China (the central institution for all transactions--from major industrial loans to individual savings accounts)

(35% of Huadong's teams were "advanced," 50% were "average," and 15% were "comparatively backward" in 1973.)

	Commune	Brigade	Team
	Credit Cooperative (funds supplied by commune members' deposits and by bank loans)	Branch, Credit Cooperative (which attracts most individual deposits)	(Teams borrow from the Credit Coop)
	(For loans for production or construction, Huadong borrows from the People's Bank)	(Brigades normally borrow from the People's Bank through the Credit Coop)	
	*Agricultural Tax Office (responsible to the Ministry of Finance) oversees Huadong's payment of approximately 5% of its annual harvest to the state as tax (paid in kind with grain)		*Informal credit society (hui) in which team members invest voluntarily for the privilege of borrowing in rotation
Commerce	Supply & Marketing Cooperative. (The state pays salaries of many coop workers, and the coop is responsible to the Hua County Commerce Bureau as well as to the commune Party Committee)	Branch store, Supply and Marketing Coop	*Supply and marketing points in teams distant from the brigade town
	Acts as purchasing agent for state corporations or agencies without representatives at Huadong		
	General store		
	Specialty shops		
	Drug store (Western & Chinese in 2 sections)		

Farm implements store

2 food shops

Restaurants

"Ice room" (bingshi)

Photo shop

2 bicycle/radio stores

Barber shop

Food stalls on street

*Grain & Oil-bearing Crops Procurement Station — *Grain Procurement & Marketing Station or Point — *Procurement Point (in some large teams)

Pig Procurement Station

Vegetable Procurement Station

*(Contracts with factories outside the commune) — *(Outside contracts) — *(Outside contracts)

Periodic market meets every 5 days

Black market in scarce commodities

Public security and people's militia — 1 public security officer (baowei weiyuan) dispatched to a Public Security Substation (paichusuo) to propagate state security policy. The lowest level court and jail are administered by Hua County. Huadong has the "Hua County Tuiguang People's Court," obviously a carryover from Tuiguang xiang.

	Commune	Brigade	Team
	People's Mediation Committee	People's Mediation Committee	People's Mediation Committees (3-5 members)
			(Militia undertakes some public security functions, including crop watching against thieves)
	Order Preservation Committee (zhian baowei weiyuanhui)	Order Preservation Committee (usually composed of militia members)	
	Militia *battalion (nearly 8,000 members, over 43% of them women)	Militia company	Militia platoon
		10 of these companies are distinguished as "4-good"	5,600 individuals are distinguished as "4-good" militia members
		Linong Brigade has 380 militia members ranging in age from 16-25.	
	(Militia volunteers labor for nonroutine tasks)	(Militia volunteers labor for nonroutine tasks): forest fires, land reclamation, and major construction	
Communications	Telephone switchboard	Telephone	Telephone
	Wired broadcasting station (receives wireless broadcasts from municipal and provincial stations)	Broadcasting station	
	*Small print shop (to reproduce circulars from higher levels)		
	Post office & telegraph		
		Loudspeaker	Loudspeakers
	(75% minimum literacy)		
Education	3 senior middle schools	Altogether 28 primary schools (24 of which have junior middle schools attached)	

	7,352 primary students with 323 teachers		
	2,077 junior middle students with 116 teachers		
	1,215 middle students with 53 teachers		
	21 university students		
	Agricultural-Technical College	*Political evening school for adults 3 evenings per month	
Cultural life	Cinema (1,100 seats)	Village square	
	Mobile projection team	Meeting hall	
	Theatrical troupe		
	Spare-time art and literary propaganda team	Spare-time art and literary propaganda team	Performing arts troupe
	Sports teams (basketball, pingpong & others) for competitions with outside teams. Total of all 3 levels: 753 teams with 7,565 players, two-thirds men and one-third women	Sports teams	Sports teams
		Lending library & reading room. Schools have libraries.	
		Exhibition room	
Medical care	Hospital (1958), 44 beds, 16 doctors (4 of traditional Chinese medicine, and 12 who are trained as well in Western medicine, 5 of them transferred to Huadong from Guangzhou). 13 nurses (all women).	Health station (weisheng zhan) (22 altogether)	Health worker (weisheng yuan). Performs this duty in addition to full-time work in the fields.
		"Barefoot doctors" (90 altogether, or more than 4 per brigade). Often these people work half-time at these duties & half-time in the fields.	

Commune	Brigade	Team
400-500 outpatients per day, about half children	3-4 midwives (75% of all midwives in the commune are in brigades. Most births are at home.)	
6 trucks available for use as ambulances		
Surgery. Operating room set up by a Guangzhou MD in 1965; improved in 1970. 130 major operations performed in 1970 (Caesarian sections, stomach & pancreas operations performed; lung & kidney operations referred)		
No bloodbank (list of volunteer donors is kept)		
Internal medicine		
Fractures & sprains		
Gynecology & obstetrics		
Optical prescriptions		
Dentistry		
Pediatrics		
13 mA X-ray machine		
Laboratory		
Small shop for making medicines		
Dispensary		

"Barefoot doctor" training:
6 classes held since 1969,
each with 30 students.
Doctors travel to brigade
health stations to give
additional instruction.

Public health services
("sanitary station" has staff
of 22)

(General checkup, including
TB check, held in 1970)

Family planning services
(1,525 births in Huadong in
1972. 80% of women of childbearing age use some birth
control method, ½ pill &
½ IUD)

Veterinary services

Health insurance

*Cooperative medical fund

Notes

1. Benjamin Ward, "The Chinese Approach to Economic Development," paper presented at the Research Conference on the Lessons of China's Development Experience for the Developing Countries, San Juan, Puerto Rico, January 31-February 2, 1976.

2. John G. Gurley, *China's Economy and the Maoist Strategy* (New York: Monthly Review Press, 1976), pp. 312-313.

3. Parris H. Chang, *Power and Policy in China* (University Park and London: Pennsylvania State University Press, 1975), pp. 76, 83.

4. The book by Chu Li and Tien Chieh-yun, *Inside a People's Commune* (Peking: Foreign Languages Press, 1975), is about Qiliying.

5. Theodore H. E. Chen, ed., *The Chinese Communist Regime: Documents and Commentary* (New York: Praeger, 1967), pp. 223-227.

6. *The Eleventh National Congress of the Communist Party of China (Documents)* (Peking: Foreign Languages Press, 1977), p. 123.

7. In suburban Shanghai communes in 1974, ownership of fixed assets and annual income earned were distributed as follows among the three levels:

Ownership level	Percent of total fixed assets owned	Percent of total annual income earned
Communes	34	31
Brigades	15	17
Teams	51	52
Total	100	100

That is, half of all assets and income belonged to production teams. One-third belonged to communes, and only one-sixth to brigades. See

Chang Chun-chiao, *On Exercising All-Round Dictatorship Over the Bourgeoisie* (Peking: Foreign Languages Press, 1975), pp. 7, 12.

8. Anna Louise Strong, *The Rise of the Chinese People's Communes—And Six Years After* (Peking: Foreign Languages Press, 1964), p. 175.

9. Mr. Xiao related this account to Professor Andrew Nathan of Columbia University in July 1973.

10. This report comes from John Burns's informant, "NM10." This person had been a work team leader in 1964 in the "four clean-ups" campaign to correct improper practices in the management of commune accounts, granaries, property, and workpoints.

11. Author's own interview, San Francisco, August 1977.

12. "Tao Zhu Is the Vanguard in Promoting Contracting Production Down to the Household—An Investigation into the Crime of Tao Zhu in Enforcing the Responsibility System of Rewards for Production in Excess of Quota at Huadong Commune," by 10,000 Li East Wind of Red Flag of Sun Yat-sen University under Red Headquarters of Guangzhou Combined Committee for Criticism of Tao Zhu, in *Nanfang ribao* [*Southern Daily*] (Guangzhou), July 26, 1967. This is translated in *Survey of China Mainland Press,* No. 4011 (August 29, 1967), pp. 14-23. Information here about Tao Zhu's activities at Huadong is taken from this article except as otherwise noted.

13. This information comes from Burns's informant, "NM10."

14. The People's Republic of China exports several English-language magazines giving official interpretations of Chinese life and policies. The most accessible ones are *China Pictorial, China Reconstructs, Chinese Literature,* and *Peking Review.*

15. James E. Nickum, *Hydraulic Engineering and Water Resources in the People's Republic of China,* Report of the U.S. Water Resources Delegation (Stanford, Calif.: Stanford University, United States-China Relations Program Report No. 2, 1977), pp. 52-53.

16. Ibid., p. 36. These data originate from James Nickum's interview with Shao Yingpiao, deputy chairman of the Huadong Revolutionary Committee, on August 21, 1974.

17. *Renmin ribao* [People's Daily], January 24, 1973.

18. Ibid., May 9, 1976.

19. Andrew Nathan, New York State Educators' Study Group.

20. Claude Aubert, "People's Communes—How to Use the Standard Visit," *New Left Review,* no. 89 (January-February 1975), p. 94.

21. "Bring the Role of Women into Full Play in Revolution and Construction," *Hongqi* [Red Flag] , no. 10 (September 1, 1971). This is translated in *Survey of China Mainland Magazines,* October 1971, pp. 73-88.

22. Chou Keh-chou, "How Our Village Got Equal Pay for Equal Work," *China Reconstructs* 24, no. 3 (March 1975), pp. 6-9. Chou's [Zhou's] village is located east of Beijing.

23. *Teaching About the People's Republic of China, Part II, A Guide for Ninth Grade Social Studies* (Albany: The University of the State of New York, the State Education Department, Bureau of Secondary Curriculum Development, 1975).

24. An unofficial text of these regulations can be found in *Documents of the Chinese Communist Party Central Committee, September 1956-April 1969*, vol. 1 (Hongkong: Union Research Institute, 1971), pp. 695-725.

25. Parris H. Chang, *Power and Policy in China*, p. 143.

26. Dwight H. Perkins, "Constraints Influencing China's Agricultural Performance," in U.S. Congress, Joint Economic Committee, *China: A Reassessment of the Economy*, 94th Cong., 1st sess., 10 July 1975, p. 358.

27. Ibid., p. 364.

28. Ibid.

DATE DUE			